Interest Groups in the
United States

INTEREST GROUPS
IN THE
UNITED STATES

GRAHAM K. WILSON

CLARENDON PRESS · OXFORD
1981

Oxford University Press, Walton Street, Oxford OX2 6DP
London Glasgow New York Toronto
Delhi Bombay Calcutta Madras Karachi
Kuala Lumpur Singapore Hong Kong Tokyo
Nairobi Dar es Salaam Cape Town
Melbourne Auckland
and associate companies in
Beirut Berlin Ibadan Mexico city

Published in the United States by
Oxford University Press, New York

British Library Cataloguing in Publication Data

Wilson, Graham K.
    Interest groups in the United States
    1. Pressure groups— United States
    I. Title
    822.4'3'0973   JK1118

    ISBN 0-19-827425-4
    ISBN 0-19-876095-7

Phototypesetting by Parkway Group,
London and Abingdon
Printed in Great Britain
at the University Press, Oxford
by Eric Buckley
Printer to the University

For Gina

Preface

Twenty-five years ago, the study of interest groups seemed likely to be one of the main branches of political science. The growing awareness of interest groups which scholars showed could be viewed as one of the most promising developments in the discipline. The study of interest groups would free political science from the strait jacket of the study of political institutions and constitutions; interest groups were part of the substance of real politics, not the arid principles of constitutional law. Above all, the study of interest groups would bridge the gap between the study of politics and the study of society. Research on interest groups promised an opportunity to assess the relative power of sectors of society through measuring their ability to shape government policies to their advantage. The reasonable assumption that interest-group activity explained many of the answers to the questions 'Who gets what, how, and when', which Lasswell had sought to place at the centre of the discipline, made their study crucial for political science. Moreover, and somewhat unusually, research on interest groups would be theoretically interesting. Greater knowledge of interest-group activity would contribute to debates in political theory about representation and would help disputes between élite and pluralist theorists about whether power is concentrated or widely dispersed.

In practice, however, studies of interest groups in the United States have been surprisingly few. The reasons for this limited development of the area are varied. The early studies of American interest groups seemed to suggest that the topic was not particularly important because the power of interest groups in the USA had been much exaggerated. It was soon established that interest groups could not switch blocks of votes from party to party. In the late 1950s it also became established that even at the national level in their activities in Washington DC, interest groups were poorly organized, lacking in prestige or expertise, concerned more with institutional survival rather than the exercise of power, and regarded with more contempt than fear by politicians. The studies of interest groups typically concentrated on relations with Congress rather than with the Executive and usually argued that legislators had far more autonomy from outside pressures than expected and were more concerned about norms or power relations within Congress than about pressure from outside.

The study of interest groups was also undermined by broader developments in political and social thought. In brief, these developments shook the belief that the study of interest groups was likely to help to answer the important questions about politics, as had been supposed. In particular, it was argued that the observable activities of interest groups did not explain the distribution of power in society or even how groups were treated by government. Control of the political agenda so that awkward issues were not raised, the prevailing ideologies which help some groups and hinder others and the power of business arising from the nature of market economies were all seen as more important than interest-group activities in explaining the distribution of power. Interesting questions about the relative power of groups seemed to require sociological rather than political-science answers.

I have attempted to come to terms with these issues in the first chapter of this book. Obviously, someone who has written a book on interest groups is likely to argue that their study is worth while. I am no exception, and would offer three justifications. First, to the extent that the early studies of interest groups in the United States were correct in their conclusions that interest groups in the United States were poorly developed, they were pointing to an unusual feature of the American political system which deserves continuing attention. In most Western democracies, interest groups have come to play a more conspicuously important role in government. 'Tri-partite' or 'neo-corporatist' ties between government, labour, and business have been detected in most northern-European countries. If

American interest groups remain weak and poorly organized, this is an important aberrant feature of the American political system which deserves close attention.

A second justification for the study of American interest groups is that although their power was much exaggerated before the empirical studies of the 1950s, interest groups remain a conspicuous part of the policy-making process in the USA. Even high-ranking politicians—such as President Carter—who begin their terms of office ignoring interest groups usually change their approach with greater experience. Indeed, most commentators and politicians in the United States believe that interest groups are more important political actors today than they have been for some time. Interest groups have become more active and better organized at the very time that other political actors, particularly parties, have become weaker.

It is the changing pattern of interest-group activity that I see as the third and most important justification for the continuing study of interest groups in the USA. Political scientists have come to recognize that in many respects the American political system is not static but changing. Political parties, Congress, the Presidency, and the electorate today all require a description different from that of twenty-five years ago, and so do interest groups. The picture of interest groups to be presented in this book is not uniform. Some will match the picture of interest groups presented by scholars in the 1950s as poorly organized and ineffective. Others will seem far more effective, and certainly highly organized. In general, however, I believe that there is a trend for interest groups to become more efficient and more effective. The intensity and competence of interest-group activity today are in general far greater than apparently was the case twenty-five years ago. Ironically, it seems, interest groups have become more important in politics at the same time as their importance to political scientists has declined.

This book is the result of some ten years' study of different American interest groups. During that time I have incurred many debts of gratitude to the officials of different interest groups, politicians, and colleagues at the Universities of Essex and Wisconsin-Madison. Above all, however, I should thank the Nuffield Foundation who have funded most of my field-work in the USA.

Contents

Interest Groups and Political Science

Interest groups have become one of the standard areas of study for political scientists; no study of a political system is complete without a section about them. There are a variety of reasons for this interest in the topic. The study of interest groups seemed one way in which political science could advance beyond the confines of studies of institutions and begin to explore the links between politics and society. Moreover, debates about interest groups quickly raised important normative issues. To some writers, interest groups are an invaluable method for supplementing elections and political parties as a means of representation and expression. Whereas political parties must (except perhaps in multi-party systems) concern themselves with broad issues and policies of importance to large groups of voters, interest groups can focus on narrower, more specialized concerns which might otherwise be neglected. Other defenders of interest groups have seen them as a valuable means by which the political system can be stabilized. Tocqueville[1] in the nineteenth century and Kornhauser[2] in the twentieth both argued that interest groups were a means by which the isolation and alienation of the individual could be avoided. A state that possesses many interest groups is a stable state. Other writers have taken a critical attitude to interest groups[3] or 'special interests', seeing in them 'caterpillars of the Commonwealth' growing fat at the expense of the public interest. Interest groups are the means by which strongly motivated minorities can overcome the will of the majority. Thus interest groups are seen as both aids and barriers to effective participation by citizens in politics.

Debates about the degree to which interest groups improve

the representativeness of the political system are linked to debates about the distribution of power in society. After all, there is little that interest groups can do to improve the representativeness of a political system if the groups themselves are grossly unequal in power, or organize only interests already well represented in the political system. Political science concerns itself with issues other than the representativeness of political systems, however. Lasswell[4] once declared that political science was the study of who gets what, how, and when. Traditionally, political scientists have seen the activities of interest groups as one of the prime answers to the questions Lasswell raised. Through campaign contributions, lobbying, and encouraging bidding for their members' votes interest groups were supposed to play a major role in shaping public policy. In no country were interest groups thought to play a more important role than in the United States.

The proposition that interest groups are particularly important in the United States can be traced back to some of the earliest writings on American politics and society. In his classic *Democracy in America,* Tocqueville argued that the energy, self-reliance, and culture of the United States combined to make interest groups much more common there than in either France or Britain. Tocqueville wrote:

In no country in the world has the principle of association been more extensively used or applied to a greater number of objects than in America . . . . In the United States, associations are established to promote the public safety, commerce, industry, morality and religion. There is no end which the human will despairs of attaining through the combined power of individuals willed or united into a common society.[5]

However, the discovery of the importance of interest groups in America preceded both Tocqueville and the Republic itself. In an oft-quoted and misquoted paper, Madison argued that one of the fundamental tasks of the new state would be the regulation of conflict between contending interests.

A landed interest, a manufacturing interest, a mercantile interest, a moneyed interest with many lesser interests grow up of necessity in civilised nations and divide themselves into different classes actuated by different sentiments and views. The regulation of these various and interfering interests forms the principal task of modern legislation and involves the spirit of party and faction in the necessary and ordinary operations of government.[6]

More recent writers have argued that the importance of interest groups in the United States is to be explained not only in terms of a greater willingness amongst Americans to participate, but also in terms of the relative weakness of divisions in the United States which in other societies provide such a strong organizing framework for politics that the scope left to interest groups is reduced. The impact of class on politics in the United States is confused and mild. Even in voting behaviour, social class in the USA is a poorer predictor of political attitudes or behaviour than it is in Scandinavia or Britain. Sharp ideological divisions which at times in other countries have created a 'society within society', such as the German Social Democrats before 1914 or the contemporary French Communist Party have been absent in the USA. Even regional loyalties, much weaker today than in the past, do not stand in the way of the influence of interest groups. It is easy to suppose that the American voter, unencumbered by class or ideology, will respond to the political arguments emanating from his interest group. The ever weaker political parties in the United States may also be expected to prove no barrier to interest-group power. Indeed, candidates may well find that interest groups are a more promising source of organizational support and campaign contributions, as well as of votes, than the moribund party organization. Finally, political scientists often suggest that the fragmentation of responsibility for Departments and agencies between the President and Congressional committees, typically composed of legislators dominated by an interest group, provides interest groups with an important opportunity to penetrate the structure of government itself. Government agencies often find that their work is supervised more closely by the Congressional committees which provide their funds and necessary legislation than by the White House. The Congressional tradition of placing Representatives and Senators on committees handling legislation or appropriations related to their constituents' interests places in a powerful position over agencies legislators themselves elected, in part, by people who are the agency's customers or 'clients'. This can give agencies an incentive to worry more about their clients than about the policies of the Chief Executive in the White House.[7]

Whether or not the factual analysis relied upon to support these arguments is sound is debatable. Indeed, we shall question the arguments or assumptions that American interest groups are particularly powerful or successful. In many respects, such as the proportion of potential members they recruit, their degree of disunity, and the seriousness with which they are taken by politicians, American interest groups look somewhat less impressive than many of their counterparts in Europe. None the less, the common assumption that interest groups in the USA are unusually powerful and important is so widespread that it provides a further reason for examining them.

The Study of Interest Groups

It is symptomatic of the confusion which bedevils the study of interest groups that there is no agreement on the definition of the term itself. Political scientists have disputed whether the better term is 'pressure' or 'interest' group, and some have suggested that the term 'interest group' should be reserved for economic groups such as business or labour. Attempts to establish differences between 'interest' and 'pressure' groups have usually been based on claims that interest groups are concerned with hard, material goals, while pressure groups are concerned with less self-interested, more altruistic goals and policies. Such distinctions are not worth maintaining. As we shall see, in practice many 'economic' groups pursue broad goals, little related to the immediate interests of their members, while many 'cause' groups pursue goals which have important economic implications. Greater concern should be paid to differentiating interest groups from other political organizations and their environment. The term 'interest group' has been used to refer to broad groups of people to whom a common interest can be ascribed (such as intellectuals or managers in the Soviet Union or young people in the West). Others have applied the term to government Departments and agencies. Such a broad application of the term robs it of its value. It is difficult to study interest groups if we use a definition which fails to distinguish them from many other forms of political life.

At heart, we know the essential elements of a definition of interest group. It is an organization which seeks or claims to represent people or organizations which share one or more common interests or ideals. An interest group may be distinguished quite easily from the *interest* it seeks to represent because it is an organization with membership lists, officers, and subscriptions which only a proportion of the potential members, the people with the shared interest, join. If only by use of government organization manuals, interest groups can also be distinguished from government agencies and Departments. It is more difficult to distinguish interest groups rigidly from political parties. It is conventional to suggest that the difference between interest groups and political parties is that political parties seek to constitute the government, whereas interest groups try only to influence it. This definition works very badly in multi-party systems such as the Netherlands or even Sweden, where—as the name implies—the Farmers' Party was an off-shoot of a pressure group. Even in the United States, which is a two-party system, the interest groups are not always distinguished easily from political parties. Interest groups perform many of the functions of political parties such as campaigning, providing political candidates with organization, funds, and publicity. In Minnesota the links between two interests and the Democratic Party were so close that the party itself is called the Democratic Farmer Labor Party. In view of this, perhaps all that can be done to distinguish political parties from interest groups is to suggest that their ostensible purpose is always narrower than that of political parties. In practice, so long as we do not use the term 'interest group' to refer to political or governmental organizations that are customarily given other labels, and use the term to refer to organizations rather than to broad sections of the population, we shall experience little difficulty. No one is likely to suggest that any of the organizations we shall look at in this book are not interest groups.

The Power of Interest Groups

If we were content to study merely the structure and activities of interest groups, we should arouse little controversy. Describing the number of officials, offices, the size, and even the quality of an interest group's publications would cause few problems. It would also arouse little interest. There is little point in studying interest groups unless we are prepared to argue that an interest group is, or is not, powerful, or even that it is more or less powerful than other interest groups. Most of our curiosity about interest groups is linked to questions about their ability to influence government policies to the advantage of their members.

Unfortunately, political scientists are deeply divided about how to go about assessing the power of interest groups. Indeed some theorists contend that the concept of power itself is an 'essentially contested concept'[8] on which there can be no agreement because disputes about its proper application are linked to differences over values and even conceptions of human nature amongst the protagonists. Other theorists contend that this view is unduly pessimistic, and that there is nothing about power which makes it more—or less—essentially contested than any other concept, including the idea of an essentially contested concept itself.

For many years the study of power seemed a relatively simple enterprise. A number of studies sought to examine the distribution of power within communities in the United States. Of these studies, the most influential was Robert Dahl's study of New Haven, *Who Governs?*[9] Dahl contended that in a relatively open system such as that prevailing in New Haven, any group with a serious problem, grievance, or goal would make it known. Dahl then argued that the observer could see whether a group was powerful or not as 'a test of overt or covert influence is the frequency with which it [he] successfully initiates policy over the opposition of others or vetoes policies initiated by others or initiates a policy where no opposition appears.' Using this technique to study a variety of policy issues, Dahl concluded that power in the community was widely diffused. No group other than the elected politicians was significant in all the issue areas, but many enjoyed some success.

Dahl's work has unleashed a storm of criticism over the years since it first appeared, partly because of genuine intellectual differences and partly because radicals found unpalatable his denial that New Haven was ruled by an élite or ruling class. One of the peculiarities of the debate that followed was that both defenders and critics of Dahl's 'pluralist' conclusions rested their arguments on analyses of power within towns which, even had there been a national élite or ruling class, would scarcely have engaged its attention. However, the terms of the debate were such as to have relevance for the discussion of the power of interests at any level of politics.

Dahl's critics can be grouped under the labels of the 'non-decisionists', the 'false consciousness' school, and the 'structuralists'. The non-decisionists, so labelled because of their stress on the importance of issues not discussed within the political arena, started from E. E. Schattschneider's[10] observation that groups are affected by the mobilization of bias. Not only do interest groups differ in the tangible resources such as money at their disposal; they differ also in the way in which they are regarded by society. In the United States, for example, there was until recently a tendency to regard trade unions with grave suspicion and business with respect. Even relatively uncontentious proposals from unions would encounter greater difficulty than proposals from businessmen of a more debatable value. (In more recent years the public has come to distrust both businessmen and unions.) Other groups, such as the poor, were so lacking in political power that they had no way of forcing consideration of their views. The allocation of resources and the values ascribed to different groups might mean that consideration of their wishes or interests never took place within the political arena. An analysis of the distribution of power based on an analysis of decisions would provide a misleading picture. The most powerless would not be those who did least well in having their proposals adopted; they would be those whose wishes or interests were never considered at all. The two originators of 'non-decision' theory, Bachrach and Baratz[11] have suggested that the poor in Baltimore constitute such a group.

The most interesting attempt to study the indirect exercise of power in 'non decisions' however is Matthew Crenson's[12] study of the politics of air-pollution control. Starting with the plausible assumption that we prefer clean air and thus good health to bad, Crenson attributes the slower speed with which one of two similar towns adopts air-pollution controls to its dominance by one company. In Gary, Indiana, which was a company town founded by its dominant employer, US Steel, the issue of pollution control was slow to emerge and never securely placed on the political agenda. In East Chicago, which in contrast had a larger number of employers, the air-pollution issue was placed on the political agenda, and after a pluralist decision-making process, an air-pollution-control ordinance was passed which would produce a significant, if temporary, decline in pollution levels.

Unfortunately, Crenson's attribution of the differences between the two towns to a non-decision-making process may not be adequate. Gary was a growing town—its population had risen by a third since World War II—and its inhabitants may well have been inclined, particularly if they were newcomers, to accept the adage that was once popular in the north of England: 'Where there's muck there's brass, [money]'. Indeed, Crenson himself notes that the town's top elected official, the Mayor, was indifferent to the pollution issue because when he saw smoke coming from the chimneys of the steel mill, he knew that there was prosperity in Gary. Thus the inhabitants of Gary may well have been more prepared to risk the greater incidence of ill health that pollution causes in return for this prosperity. Whether we think the Mayor's view is commendable is immaterial; it is a perfectly plausible view to hold, and to assert that the air-pollution issue *should* have been raised is to impose our own preferences on the situation, something political scientists try to avoid as long as possible.

An even more fundamental criticism of the pluralist theory and approach has been made by Steven Lukes.[13] Whereas Bachrach and Baratz had contended that certain groups were unable to have their interests taken seriously, Lukes contended that the most powerful groups were able to protect their interests by controlling how members of a society conceptualize their interests. A critical attitude to the interests of the most powerful group thus never develops. Obviously, the most desirable position for business is not merely having competent lobbyists in Washington; it is living in a society which believes that what is good for General Motors is good for the United States. Though there may be the occasional dispute about the design of a new car or the location of a factory, the fundamental interests of business would not be challenged because no one would be able to see any point in doing so, or even imagine what such a challenge would look like. It is easy to see why Lukes's concept of power inclines him to the view that the concept itself is essentially contested. For Lukes's approach requires him to decide externally what the interests of groups or individuals are, even if the people to whom he ascribes these interests are unaware of them. If workers do not show any signs of wanting to overthrow capitalism it is not because they have decided that the risks of upheaval are too great or the rewards of a socialist society unalluring; it is because their conceptual framework has been warped by capitalist society in its most blatant exercise of power. As Barry[14] has pointed out, Lukes also seems caught in a contradiction in that he argues that the concept of power is essentially contested, depending on personal beliefs and values, while at the same time he also argues that his approach to the study of power is better than that of the pluralists or even of Bachrach and Baratz.

A final sort of objection to the pluralism of Dahl's early writings comes from those who emphasize the structural constraints which operate on those in authority. According to this view, the clash between consumer and labour interest groups, like all politics, takes place within the setting of a market economy whose requirements impose limitations or constraints on governments. These limitations will be taken into account by government without any political pressure from companies. This argument was, somewhat unexpectedly, stated by Charles Lindblom in his lucid book, *Politics and Markets*.[15] Lindblom, previously associated with conservative views, argued that business groups occupied a 'privileged position' far different from those of other interest groups. This is because in capitalist societies businessmen are entrusted with the making of decisions which determine the level of prosperity which cities, regions, and even whole nations enjoy. If businessmen feel that a government is indifferent or hostile to the needs and privileges of business, executives will be less inclined to invest; slower economic growth and lower employment will ensue. 'Business confidence' is something all governments in capitalist societies must maintain if their citizens are to prosper. Government is required to provide what businessmen need in order to perform their functions on behalf of society.

In the eyes of the government officials, therefore, businessmen do not appear simply as representatives of a special interest, as representatives of interest groups do, they appear as functionaries performing functions that government officials regard as indispensable. When a government official asks himself whether business needs a tax deduction he knows that he is asking a question about the welfare of the whole society and not simply about a favour to that segment of that population which is what is typically at stake when he asks himself should he respond to an interest group.[16]

Government officials do not need to be pressured by businessmen in the same ways as by other interests. The government official who knows the realities of life in market economies will see the need to agree to business's demands.

He does not have to be bribed, duped or pressured to do so. Nor does he have to be an uncritical admirer of businessmen to do so. He simply understands, as is plain to see, that public affairs in market oriented systems are in the hands of two groups of leaders, government and business, and that to make the system work, government leadership must often defer to business leadership.[17]

Lindblom notes that governments will not always defer to business, but that disputes with businessmen have costs; agreements with them, in contrast, have benefits. For example, 40 per cent of the investment carried out in the USA in 1963 was attributed to a 1962 tax concession on new investment.

The 'structuralist' analysis of power is open to objection, too. Businessmen often have not known their own interests. For example, President Franklin D. Roosevelt is often described today as the person who, through his New Deal policies, saved American capitalism. Yet businessmen at the time Roosevelt was President regarded him as the destroyer of the capitalist system, a traitor to the wealthy classes from which he came. Similarly, politicians do not appreciate the effects of their policies on business as readily as Lindblom suggests; right-wing politicians in Britain and the United States have often unwittingly launched policies harmful to business. In short, the constraints on politicians which a market system imposes are not as easily perceived as Lindblom suggests. Moreover, how far business interests are able to rely on their structural importance in the economy to influence politics varies too. There are times when the business community has few critics and therefore little need to organize politically: there are other occasions when business interests are more vigorously challenged, and are likely to respond with more vigorous defence of their interests through political action.

The problem for the student of interest groups is obvious. Whichever concept of power he accepts, he will lay himself open to the charge that he has misunderstood the true basis of power. Those who adopt a pluralist approach concentrating on observable conflicts will be accused of missing the more important, veiled exercise of power in keeping issues off the political agenda completely by controlling the ideology of society. Arguments based on 'non-decisions' seem to have the advantage of allowing for the empirical identification of issues which have some support but are not on the political agenda. Even this is difficult, however. Public opinion is often vague, transitory, and inconsistent. The same voters frequently favour tax cuts on the one hand and increases in the government programmes taxes pay for on the other. In so far as the public is aware of issues, it focuses frequently on issues and topics which have been promoted or popularized by politicians and the media. We are unlikely to find in the electorate preferences for coherent policies which are neglected totally by politicians. To go further and decide, as Lukes would have us do, that certain causes should be popular politically, though they are not present, is a temptation which all who think about or practise politics yield to from time to time. Yet it is something which is difficult to defend as any more than an indirect statement of our values and prejudices. There are many who argue that were it not for our ideological conditioning we should all be working for the overthrow of capitalism and the establishment of a socialist commonwealth. There are those, too, who argue that were the truth not suppressed by politicians and the media we should be extending the hand of friendship to the inhabitants of other planets. Such debatable views seem a risky starting-point for research.

The debate over approaches to the study of power has been more successful in pointing to weaknesses in approaches than in bringing approaches to the discipline. Unless we are prepared to suspend all enquiry into interest groups and possibly other phenomena until that distant day when political theorists have settled on a definition of power, empirical political scientists must do the best they can to avoid the pitfalls that the theorists have either warned us of, or perhaps even dug. Perhaps there are reasons why the traps can be avoided.

In the first place, few would claim that the observable exercising of power, the detectable aspect that Dahl focused on in his New Haven study, is totally irrelevant. If we can see that an interest group, such as a labour union, proposes a policy, such as tougher laws on occupational safety and health, it would be strange to suggest that if the union succeeds in having the policy adopted over the opposition of other interests, this does not constitute any evidence of power. On the other hand, the critics of the pluralists are on much stronger ground when they suggest that the absence of visible involvement in policy making or political debate on the part of an interest does not prove that the interest is powerless. Rather the interest group may enjoy a position which is so strong—because of the ability it enjoys to keep issues off the political agenda or because the prestige the dominant ideology accords it—that it makes political involvement impossible and unnecessary. The successful deployment of resources such as campaign contributions, lobbyists, or votes by an interest group are *an* aspect of power, as no one would deny. Debate focuses on whether the deployment of such resources is the only aspect of power, the major aspect of power, or a minor component in the picture.

A second way in which we can progress is to note that until now we have happily accepted the assumption made by the critics of the pluralists such as Bachrach and Baratz or Lukes that the greater aspect of power enjoyed by groups is the power based on ideology or on control over the political agenda. It is assumed that the more important issues are the issues which are not debated, which are not placed on the political agenda. With the obvious exception of debates about totally restructuring society, which—not surprisingly—societies rarely engage in, it might be reasonable to ask for some evidence that this is in fact the case. At the very least, there is no reason why we should suppose that an interest is the silent beneficiary of government policy because of its ideological strength until we have looked to see whether it is in fact silent in the political process. This suggests that proponents of the non-decision approach should suspend their judgement until evidence has been gathered about the extent to which the various interests do engage in politics, and on what scale. Critics of the pluralists have contended that the aspect of the power of interest groups they describe is the tip of the iceberg. We have contended that the critics of the pluralists have given us no way of knowing whether we are looking at the tip of the iceberg or the bulk of it when we see the direct attempts of interest groups to exercise power. All might agree, however, that it is desirable to assess the extent of the observable attempts interests make to exercise power.

A third way in which we can progress is to abandon the idea that the bases and distribution of power are unchanging. The degree to which interests need to form groups and involve themselves in the political process in fact varies over time. As we shall see, businessmen in the United States today feel that the greater extent of government regulation of their activities and the rise of what they regard as hostile interest groups representing consumers and environmentalists has made it imperative that they too should form interest groups and engage in more direct political action. This is quite a change from the situation in the 1950s when business interests were almost unchallenged. Eisenhower's Secretary of Defense could argue that 'what is good for the country is good for General Motors and vice versa' and the Cabinet consisted entirely of millionaires or business executives. This is not to suggest that business in the United States today is about to be nationalized. It is to suggest that business now needs to protect its interests in different ways, and perhaps more strenuously, than in the 1950s. Equally clearly, large numbers of consumers and environmentalists have decided that they have common interests which only interest groups can protect. In short, circumstances change, and as circumstances change, interests find it necessary to form groups or to adopt different tactics. An interest protected by a favourable ideological climate may not find that it is so protected for ever. All political scientists might agree, therefore, that monitoring the current level of political involvement by different interests and the changes which are taking place over time is well worth while.

This study sets out to describe the current levels of political activity of some of the major interests in American society—business, unions, farmers, consumers, environmentalists, and others who seek to represent the public interest. We shall also look at the activities of some of the numerous groups which campaign on issues ranging from the Panama Canal Treaties to abortion. In undertaking this survey it will not be assumed that the directly observable exercise of political power is, as the pluralists suggested, the only form of power. Indeed, we shall see that the arguments advanced by writers such as Lukes or Bachrach and Baratz help us to make sense out of a number of apparent paradoxes. For example, we shall see that labour unions in the United States until recently maintained a political capability far in excess of that of business, yet did much worse in terms of government policy. Merely describing the political organizations these two organizations bring to bear would not provide an accurate picture. We shall argue, however, that observing the direct attempts of these interests to influence policy is the obvious place to start. The emphasis of this book, therefore is on observable activities of interest groups in the United States. It is hoped that this focus will be defensible partly because the overt activities of interest groups are of growing importance: indeed, one of the themes of the book will be that even as the ideas of the pluralist writers such as Dahl became less fashionable, the United States was becoming a more pluralist political system. Now by this it is not meant to suggest that the United States is a political system in which all sectors of society have an approximately equal chance of influencing policy. On the contrary, there is a massive disparity between the resources that groups deploy. It is, however, to make two points about interest groups in the United States today. First, the familiar criticism of pluralism that not everyone had an interest group to represent him and that important common interests were neglected is less true today than it was once. General or public interests in a clean environment or in safe consumer goods are advanced vigorously by the public interest groups which made such an impact on Washington in the 1970s. Even major sectors of the poorest parts of the population achieved some representation by groups such as unions and civil-rights groups which adopted their cause. It is worth repeating that we shall not be arguing that ghetto dwellers have a lobby to compare with Exxon's. But a second point of note about the contemporary American interest-group scene is precisely that it is so much more comprehensive than in the past. As politicians and commentators in the United States today are wont to complain, the number of interest groups and lobbyists at work in Washington is rising constantly and rapidly. Very few interests which have the option of organizing to exert pressure fail to take it. This is far from being a trivial statement, because, as we shall see, it used not to be true. For example, the giant multinational, ITT (International Telephone and Telegraph), did not have an office in Washington to lobby on the company's behalf until as recently as 1961. Studies of business lobbyists in the 1950s found that they were poorly organized, divided, and ineffective. Perhaps for the reasons advanced by

Bachrach and Baratz or Lukes, potentially powerful groups such as business chose to sit out the political battle: they probably did not need to be involved. This has changed. Fewer groups feel able to afford to ignore politics. Again, we shall not suggest that the directly observable resources enjoyed by interest groups are their only strengths, or that the biases of the political agenda or of ideology have ceased to count. We shall suggest, however, that at least in the view of those directly involved in protecting important interests—be they labour, business, or consumers' interests—the open political battle matters. Arguably these people are in a good position to know. The American political system has changed, perhaps even developed, to the point at which powerful interests join the game, and no longer content themselves with cheering on favoured players from the sidelines.

Features of interest groups in the United States

As we examine the range of interest groups covered in this book, we shall seek to answer several questions about all of them. First, we shall want to know what interests they pursue, and how they define the interests of those they claim to represent. The answers to these questions are far from predictable. Indeed, some major interest groups appear to pursue policies contrary to the apparently obvious interests of their members. Many interest groups stray far from the concerns which we should expect them to have.

Second, we shall want to know why people with that interest have organized, and the extent to which others have joined them who share that interest. Interest groups vary according to the success they enjoy in recruiting potential members.

Third, we shall ask what success interest groups have had in establishing a sense that they are the legitimate spokesmen for the interests they claim to represent. Not every interest group that claims to speak on behalf of an interest is taken to represent it. For example, the Anti Italian American Defamation League was taken by many to represent not Italian Americans but the Mafia, particularly after one of its luminaries was gunned down in what had all the hallmarks of an inter-gang feud.

Fourth, we shall want to know how the interests in question try to influence policy. We might expect to find a marked difference between the ways different types of interest groups operate—so that mass-membership organizations such as unions behave in a very different way from a business corporation—or else we may expect to find that the need to operate in a common political system imposes relatively uniform requirements on all the groups.

Finally, we shall conclude by putting the interest groups of the United States in a comparative setting and asking what, if anything, makes them distinctively American. Do interest groups representing business or workers look much the same in the USA as in other countries? Or are there features of the interest groups of the United States which as a result of the American culture or political system make them significantly different from those elsewhere?

Selection of Interest Groups

The interest groups covered in this study have been selected not according to some scientific sampling of all known interest groups but on the basis of the interest or significance of the groups chosen. We shall start by looking at agricultural interest groups because they were the first large-scale attempts made by an important sector of the population to mobilize in order to secure government policies to offset their economic disadvantages. Though a lively interest to this day, farmers were the first of the economic interests to organize, and are worth our attention on that account. We shall then look at the political activities of business and labour. They appear in this study because it is hard to imagine that we should know much about the workings of a political system in an industrialized society if we did not take account of how these interests relate to society. Our attention will then turn to the attempts made by public interest groups to plug the more obvious holes in the interest-group system of representation by organizing consumers and those who care about the environment. Bearing in mind the growing importance which commentators attribute to such groups, we shall look at the non-economic, single issue groups which are concerned with such issues as the abortion laws or key incidents in American foreign policy such as the Panama Canal treaties signed by President Carter. Finally, we shall discuss changes in the tactics employed by interest groups and their changing role in American politics.

The Agricultural Interest Groups

American agriculture has been the recipient of massive government aid for over half a century. American farm income throughout most of the 1950s and 1960s would have been halved without the deployment by the government of a variety of techniques to subsidize farming, including payments to farmers not to produce, government purchase of commodities it thought were being sold too cheaply, and direct payments to farmers. These subsidies have been computed to be worth together some $6 billion annually.[1]

There are several reasons why agriculture has been so dependent on the government for help. Most obviously, the nature of the industry makes it extremely difficult for production to be planned at a level which will balance supply and demand at prices producing a reasonable income for farmers. Farming is carried out by many thousands of autonomous producers, each making decisions about how much to produce, co-ordinated only by price mechanisms. It is much easier for the car industry, in contrast, to avoid over-production because there are only three major producers in the USA. Moreover, the very nature of farming makes wild fluctuations in income and prices likely. The weather can have an enormous impact, turning years of scant production into years of surplus in which prices tumble and farm incomes fall. Introductory economics textbooks often show that a free market in agriculture can be perpetually unstable. High prices in one year encourage over-production and surpluses in the next; the resulting low prices and farm incomes encourage under-production, high prices, and high farm incomes the following year.[2] Government action to stabilize the market can benefit both farmers and consumers by securing steady levels of production, and holding surplus stocks off the market in years of good harvests to stabilize prices in years of scarcity.

Beyond these recurring problems of agricultural economics, the industry has been undergoing a profound change. Just before the Second World War, agriculture employed one-fifth (20 per cent) of the American population; today it employs one-twenty-fifth, (4 per cent) of the population. These changes are part of a transformation of agriculture brought about by mechanization, chemical fertilizers, and vast capital investments. The transformation of agriculture has left a small number of farmers controlling vast business enterprises, frequently worth half a million dollars. But the change was achieved by the gradual squeezing out of the industry of numerous smaller-scale farmers, who found that they could not make an adequate income in agriculture and were forced first into debt, then off the land. As the tie between a farmer and his land is usually close, the squeezing of farmers off the land was accompanied by much anguish and demands for government action to keep farm prices at a level which would secure a satisfactory income for the smaller, less efficient producer.

It is extremely doubtful whether demands that the government commit itself to arresting the tides of technological change would ever have been taken seriously. But a number of influences, including the onset of the Great Depression and the chance occurrence of surpluses due to good weather or temporary stimuli to production, such as the Second World War and Korea, disguised the nature of the farm problem. Demands were made, with apparent plausibility, that the government should secure justice for the farmer by guaranteeing farm incomes at a level often referred to as parity, a level defined as the ratio of farm to non-farm incomes in the last peacetime golden era of American agriculture, 1909–14.

Yet government intervention frequently has its costs, even for its supposed beneficiaries. In particular, to avoid in peacetime the creation of massive surpluses which the government was obliged to purchase, beneficiaries of farm subsidies have been obliged to accept controls over the amount they produced. At times, for example in the 1950s, these controls were imposed through an amusing panoply of bureaucratic controls, including spotter aircraft used to look for illicitly planted acres.[3] The cost of agricultural subsidies in short was that agriculture became dependent on political decisions, or, as some would describe it, on government interference. For half a century American farmers have seemed to be confronted with the choice between a catastrophic slump in income and a degree of government control which many of them found uncongenial. Agriculture had been deeply involved in politics for most of this century because of its economic circumstances. Of late, however, involvement has taken on new forms with the emergence of new issues such as the safety of chemical fertilizers and government regulation of their use. The American farmer has in many ways become a businessman controlling huge assets. As such, like other businessmen, he finds the presence of government more pervasive and irritating. Unlike most other businessmen, however, his industry has been massively dependent on government policies since the New Deal. Ironically, farming, that most individualistic of industries was the first to enter the collectivist age.

Because of the close involvement of government in agriculture and the frequency with which farmers have demanded government action to solve their problems, it might seem reasonable to suppose that farm interest groups are unusually long-established, well organized, and powerful. This does not seem to have been the case. Instead, the general farm groups have been divided, often dogmatic, and of surprisingly limited effectiveness. Before starting our examination of individual farm organizations, it is worth stressing one surprising fact about the agricultural interest groups collectively. In spite of the general belief that Americans join interest groups more frequently than other nationalities do, the percentage of farmers *all* the rival groups organize—often referred to as the 'density' of membership—is very low, no more than 35 per cent. This density of membership is less than that achieved by a single group in Britain, the National Farmers' Union.

The General Farm Groups

The AFBF. The American Farm Bureau Federation is by far the largest of the general farm organizations. With over 2 million members in every state but Alaska, the AFBF is the only organization with an ostensible claim to speak for all of American agriculture.

In spite of the long-established dependence of agriculture on government, the AFBF was not the result of a spontaneous movement by American farmers. The first farm bureau was created probably in Binghampton, New York, in 1911 (though some claim the honour for Pettis County, Missouri). But the development of the Farm Bureaux really began in 1914 with the passing of the Smith Lever Act which established an agricultural extension service to advise farmers on improving their methods of production. The local agents appointed to carry out this task often formed a local organization or farm bureau to help them establish the good relations with farmers that their task obviously required, and to overcome the hostility which might have attached itself to agents of the federal government. By 1915 there were enough bureaux to make state federations possible, and in 1919 a national organization was formed. In the South, the farm bureaux developed slightly differently, developing out of the committees elected by farmers to administer New Deal programmes. Here too, though, the farm bureaux were thus in effect sponsored by government agencies rather than developing spontaneously. In spite of legislation, the True–Howard Act, banning work by the Extension Service for the Farm Bureaux Federation, such activities were undoubtedly important in helping the AFBF to grow. A county agent for the Extension Service in one state sent out letters to farmers telling them that their farm-subsidy cheques were in his office, where he would be happy to enrol them in the Farm Bureau.[4] Such instances encouraged critics of the AFBF to argue that it had been 'conceived by businessmen and county agents, born in a Chamber of Commerce, nurtured on funds from industry and has never completely left its home and parents.'[5]

It is possible to argue that the conservative principles which so dominate the current policies of the AFBF have their origin in the way the AFBF developed. The spirit of the Extension Service was to encourage farmers to overcome their problems through individual effort and initiative, not through reliance on political solutions. Indeed, the encouragement of the AFBF was due partly to a fear of such radical rival movements as the populist and Non-Partisan League. Thus, the farm bureau in Illinois believed that 'it is our duty in creating this organisation to avoid any policy which will align organised farmers with the radicals of other organisations'.[6] Nationally, in spite of disagreements with merchants and meat packers, the AFBF committed itself to work 'for a better understanding of the Farmers' basic difficulties on the part of business and financial leaders'.[7] Yet the conservative tradition in the AFBF was not continuous. During the years of extreme misery which American agriculture suffered before and during the Great Depression, the Bureau worked hard to secure government programmes to help the farmer. The Bureau tried to persuade farmers to forget Al Smith's Catholicism and his opposition to prohibition and vote for him rather than for Hoover. The Bureau worked closely with Roosevelt in establishing the New Deal agricultural programmes, and tried to whip in rival Congressmen to vote for measures to benefit the depressed urban poor in exchange for help from northern liberals such as Fiorella La Guardia on agricultural issues. Only after the Second World War did the AFBF revert to deeply conservative leaders and policies.

Just as the early growth of the AFBF was not a spontaneous rival movement, so its membership today represents factors other than enthusiasm for the organization of its policies.

Many farmers join the AFBF to take advantage of services such as cheap insurance and tyres which it offers its members. More disconcertingly, a large number of people who are not farmers also join the AFBF, people who want the individualized benefits but have no interest in agriculture or agricultural policy. Critics of the Farm Bureau argue that the membership figures it claims do not reflect accurately the strength of the Farm Bureau amongst farmers because they include large numbers of non-farmers who join merely to obtain the cheap insurance and other concessions available only to members. Indeed, an enquiry by Representative Resnick (D., New York) argued that 50 per cent of the membership of the Farm Bureau were not farmers, and that in four states (Illinois, Alabama, Florida, and Indiana) the AFBF claimed more family-farm memberships than there were farms. In Cook County, Illinois— most of which is the city of Chicago and has only 1,000 farms— the AFBF claimed 7,000 members.[8]

Political scientists such as Mancur Olson[9] have argued that the only way that interest groups can attract members is by offering benefits which are available to members only, benefits such as those that the Farm Bureau offers. Olson did not, however, anticipate that organizations would stray into the recruitment of people from outside their natural constituency. The Farm Bureau itself contends that the selling of selective benefits—and thus of memberships—to people who are not farmers is essential if the farming members are to be provided with satisfactory services. Critics of the AFBF contend that the large non-farm membership has caused the organization to shift away from a concern with the problems of farming to a concern with the problems of insurance and retailing.[10] The AFBF has encouraged its affiliates to divide the membership into farming and non-farming categories. Only 'persons, partnerships, unincorporated associations and corporations actively engaged in the production of agricultural products . . . who receive a substantial proportion of their income from such products' should be allowed to vote on policies and the selection of officers, according to the Federation's rules. Yet this requirement has not been enforced in practice. In the early 1970s only one-third of state farm bureaux were limiting the right to vote to farming members. In this minority of better-organized farm bureaux which do make this distinction, the proportion of non-farming members varies from 10 to 45 per cent. As the temptation to sign up non-farmers as members may well be higher in the less-organized states, the proportion of non-farmers who are members nationally may be similar to the proportion in states with numerous non-farming members. As many members—whether they are farmers or not—join to take advantage of specific benefits, because the wide geographic dispersal of farmers in the United States and the unwillingness of ordinary members to participate in most interest groups, a tiny proportion of Farm Bureau members control their organization. Less than 10 per cent usually attend meetings or vote. Though lack of participation is by no means unusual in interest groups, people are particularly suspicious of the representatives of the Farm Bureau's leaders because of the nature of the policies they follow. In particular it is often contended that the national leaders of the AFBF use their position to push extremely conservative policies which often have little to do with agriculture, and when they do are damaging to the interests of American farmers.

It is certainly the case that the AFBF concerns itself with a wide range of topics of little direct relevance to agriculture and takes a fiercely conservative stand on most issues. For example, the AFBF has called for the expulsion of the United Nations on the grounds that it is a base for espionage, subversion, and for 'ridicule and vindictiveness against our free enterprise system and constitutional governments'. The AFBF campaigned against an amnesty for draft dodgers, measures to reduce the power of unions, and against the child-labour laws because they 'encourage idleness and juvenile delinquency'.[11] Long after American involvement in Vietnam had become unpopular in the USA, the AFBF supported 'aid for the people of Vietnam in their defence of freedom'.

The general conservatism of the AFBF is nowhere clearer than in its approach to economic policy. The AFBF takes a firm, even a dogmatic, view of the dangers of government intervention in the economy. The Farm Bureau claims that 'One of the greatest dangers threatening our republic and our system of private competitive enterprise is the apathy of the American people and the apparent lack of responsibility on the part of the individual citizen in allowing the socialisation of America.' This 'socialisation of America' covers a wide variety of policies, for 'the welfare state is based on centralisation of power in the federal government and the redistribution of the benefits of our economic system by political means and is akin to socialism and communism.' The AFBF sees no difference between property and human rights.

It would be extremely difficult for the Farm Bureau to reconcile such a philosophy with support for government intervention to raise farm incomes. Farm-price-support systems are deliberately and explicitly designed to 'redistribute the benefits of our economic system by political means'. With commendable consistency, the AFBF has always advocated sharp reductions in farm-price supports, arguing that farm-subsidy programmes should be ended 'as rapidly as possible'. After heavy criticism, the AFBF has agreed that subsidy programmes should be retained 'for three or five years' and even that government subsidies should be paid to farmers in the event of extremely rare, disastrously low prices prevailing. In 1977, bowing before the storm of grass-roots discontent over prices, the AFBF accepted the need to rescue wheat farmers from the squeeze of low prices and the high levels of debt incurred in more prosperous times. By and large, however, the AFBF has been steadfast in its opposition to farm subsidies.

The AFBF produces reasoned arguments to support its policies. It contends that artificially high prices kill demand. For example, when the US government bought cotton to raise American cotton prices, it produced a situation in which competitors in other countries could take away American export markets. Moreover, the AFBF is certainly right to point out that in order to limit their cost, subsidies are usually accompanied by stringent and irksome controls, limiting the freedom to produce whatever farmers wish in as large a quantity as they can, which most farmers prize. Unless subsidies for commodities are balanced carefully, help for the producer of one commodity, e.g. feed grains, will hurt the producers of another, e.g. cattle or chicken farmers. Many farm commodities are not sold to consumers but to other farmers. Yet few farmers are prepared to live in a totally free market, particularly as to do so, according to all the best economic studies of American agricultural programmes, would lead to a reduction of 50 per cent in their incomes. American farmers producing commodities as diverse as cotton, tobacco, and wheat have shown, by enrolling in programmes in which subsidies are given in exchange for limiting their production and by almost invariably approving mandatory controls in referenda of producers, that they do not share the AFBF's attitude to subsidy programmes. Surveys conducted by both social scientists and journalists suggest that most AFBF members share the belief of most of the farm organizations that farmers need strong government programmes to protect their incomes.[12] Not surprisingly, most farmers have no desire to be much poorer.

The rigid attachment of the AFBF's leadership to extreme *laissez-faire* views has prompted a number of grass-roots rebellions. In 1960 the *laissez-faire* leadership of the Illinois branch of the AFBF was defeated on a rank-and-file revolt. However, there are surprisingly few signs of overt conflict in the AFBF. The central authorities of the AFBF have so little power over state bureaux that the constitution provides for formal 'dissents' in which the state bureaux, if they disapprove of a national policy, can formally dissociate themselves from it. Yet in practice the procedure is rarely used because the state and county bureaux can go their own way without interference. State farm bureaux even testify in Washington in favour of proposals fundamentally at odds with official national policy. Representatives and Senators find frequently that local branches are opposed to the policies of the AFBF. As one remarked to the AFBF President,

This last fall and every fall I go around to various counties. In almost every county a delegate of your organisation comes to call on me. For fifteen minutes they give me the policy of the AFBF, then they say 'that is the official position of the AFBF. Now we want to tell you what we think'.[13]

The current chairman of the House Agriculture Committee, Tom Foley (D., Washington), once remarked that 'national policies [of the AFBF] do not often find a reflection in local agricultural areas . . . These individual Farm Bureaux have not taken the positions of hostility to the farm programmes that have been reflected on the national level.'[14] One of his Republican colleagues agreed, and added: 'We do sense a tremendous difference in the attitude of individual members of the Farm Bureau from the position taken by the American Farm Bureau.'[15]

The Influence of the AFBF. In spite of its size, the AFBF does not enjoy widespread respect in Washington DC. Its habit of having an opinion on almost every conceivable subject destroys any pretensions it may have had to being a group with peculiar expertise on farm policy. Moreover, its heavily ideological style offends legislators who might have been its allies. The bulk of the Democrats, and a liberal minority in the Republican Party, are not inclined to accept the claim made by one of the AFBF's Presidents that 'Economic laws . . . are as surely God-given as are the great truths which have been recorded and demonstrated in the Bible. There is a law of supply and demand which constitutes an economic truth as well as a basic moral law.'[16]

Moreover, as we have seen, Representatives and Senators know that the national leadership of the AFBF is not representing the views of a majority of American farmers. Representative Cooley once told a President of the AFBF testifying before the Agriculture Committee when Cooley was its Chairman: 'You are speaking for my farmers but you are not having any effect on me.'[17]

However, policies favoured by the AFBF have on occasion been enacted. Thus the 1973 Agriculture Act cut back on farm subsidies and left farmers more or less dependent on market forces. As the Act was passed at a time when the world demand for farm products was unusually high, it had little adverse effect of farm incomes until 1976. In 1976 and 1977, grain prices fell rapidly, and formidable pressure developed in rural America for the reintroduction of subsidies. This took place with the 1977 Act, which even the AFBF was forced to agree was necessary. When the AFBF has secured a shift in government policy in the direction it usually favours, of fewer controls and no subsidies, it succeeds not because of its own power or persuasiveness but because of the congruence between its views and those of Republican Secretaries of Agriculture. Eisenhower, Nixon, and Ford have usually appointed Agriculture Secretaries with as dogmatic a belief in the free market as the AFBF's. (Only Clifford Hardin, who was sacked by Nixon after two years was more moderate.) Though the policies of such Republican Secretaries as Ezra Taft Benson (1952–60) have usually been very unpopular with farmers, they have won the approval of AFBF leaders. In turn, the AFBF leaders have ready access to the Agriculture Department when the Republicans are in office. It is doubtful if they had much expertise, information, or advice worth communicating.

The National Farmers' Union (NFU). Though third in size of the general farm organizations, with a membership around 250,000, the NFU is at least equal in status to the AFBF. This may well be because it is the very antithesis of the AFBF in terms of its views, policies, and traditions. Though the NFU was founded in Texas in 1902, its main strength is in the upper midwest and the wheat-producing areas of the west. The reason for the change is probably that the leadership of the NFU has been as determinedly liberal as the AFBF has been conservative. The NFU has supported as wide a range of causes as the AFBF, but from the opposite point of view. The Union opposed the Supersonic Transport and American involvement in the Vietnam War, while supporting the War on Poverty, and a more generous policy on Social Security payments. These were all well-known liberal causes. In farm policy, the NFU favours government intervention as strongly as the AFBF favours a free market. Accepting the analysis of the contemporary American economy put forward by Galbraith,[18] the NFU argues that farmers are at a special disadvantage.

The United States . . . has a 'mixed' economy in which the free market has been modified and circumvented in various ways, by corporate structures for business, by tariffs and import restrictions, by laws for fair price trading and fair competition, by exclusive franchises and on assured return on investment for utilities, by restriction on entry into certain trades and professions, and by collective bargaining for workers. The family farmer stands virtually alone as a textbook example of free competition in the US economy.[19]

Whereas the AFBF may deplore these developments and seek to reverse them, the NFU supported them to ensure justice for the farmer within this context through the intervention of the Federal government.

The liberalism of the NFU puzzles many observers who associate farmers more with conservatism than with liberalism, and the upper midwest with McCarthyism rather than with compassion. Of course, many of the NFU's members have as little interest in its policies as the AFBF's members have in that organization. Many join to take advantage of grain elevators or Blue Cross–Blue Shield health-insurance schemes reserved for NFU members. Moreover, there is no evidence to suggest that members of the NFU differ materially from members of the AFBF. Both organizations recruit predominantly from the ranks of the richest farmers, in spite of the NFU's image of defending the 'family farmer'. In his excellent study of the NFU, Crampton[20] shows that it is impossible to distinguish members of the NFU from the members of the AFBF on the basis of income or of the sort of crop they produce. Neither the common belief that the NFU is an organization of small farmers nor the belief that the liberalism of the organization is explained by the peculiar character of wheat production fits the facts.

On the other hand, it is surely more than coincidence that this most liberal of all farm organizations flourishes in a part of the United States which has had a liberal political tradition. It is well known that the upper-mid-western states were important bases of populism and progressivism. Many well-known writers such as Hofstadter, Shils, and Lipset[21] have suggested that there is a reactionary, intolerant character to populism which surfaced in the aftermath of World War II as McCarthyism. More recent—and more careful—scholarship has cast doubt on this view.[22] Populism itself was a radical, but not an irrational, creed: the areas which had backed progressives such as La Follettes voted not for, but against, McCarthy, partly because of a party realignment in the region which carried the progressives into the Democratic Party.

The general liberalism of the NFU and its support for active farm programmes give it a close relationship with the Democrats. Democrats are much more likely than Republicans—even than rural Republicans—to support farm-subsidy programmes. Even if Republicans do support the NFU's farm programmes, they are unlikely to be rated very highly by the NFU because of their views on non-farm issues. Thus all the Senators who were 100 per cent correct in the NFU's evaluation of voting records are Democrats. Where a state in which NFU is strong—such as North Dakota—sends one Republican and one Democratic Senator to Washington, the NFU views them very differently, giving the Republican (Young) a low score on his voting record (43 per cent) and the Democrat (Burdick) 87 per cent. The NFU, though officially non-partisan, frequently distributes anti-Republican literature in Presidential election years (e.g. 1972) and at the local level is well integrated into Democratic Party structure. Indeed, in North Dakota, the NFU played a major role in creating the Democratic Party in a state in which the Republicans had always predominated. The NFU has also functioned as a source of recruits for the Department of Agriculture when the Democrats are in office, supplying several Under and Assistant Secretaries of Agriculture. In turn, the NFU has employed some prominent Democratic former officials of the USDA, including Charles Brannan, Truman's Secretary of Agriculture. Relations between the NFU and the Department of Agriculture are close when the Democrats are in power, and more distant when the Republicans are in office. Relations with the Democratic legislators are always good, but the NFU is less likely to arouse the antagonism of the Congressional Republicans than the AFBF is to court the wrath of the Democrats.

Nevertheless, in some ways the organizations are mirror images. Just as the AFBF is thought to be too preoccupied with conservative issues of little direct relationship to agriculture, so the NFU is thought to focus on too many liberal, non-agricultural issues. Like the AFBF, the NFU has effective ties to only one part of the political community and has limited quantities of the politically neutral, technocratic expertise at which many European interest groups aim. And, like the Farm Bureau, the NFU can hope to see its policies adopted only when forces outside its control bring its friends to power. Yet herein lies an important difference. Whereas the AFBF can influence national policy only when the Republicans control the Administration, the NFU's friends, the Democrats, have controlled Congress continuously since 1954 and are expected to continue to do so. Though the NFU's best contacts are with the liberal Democrats, it has reasonable relations with Southern Democrats too. In that sense it is never as powerless as the AFBF is when the Democrats control both the legislative and executive. Moreover, the doubts about the representativeness of its policies are fewer. The NFU, while limited in influence, is less so than the AFBF, whose reputation is altogether more dubious.

The Grange. The last of the comprehensive farm groups is the Grange. Though the oldest and the second largest, it is also the least consequential. This is because in many ways the Grange has become more of a social organization characterized by odd ritual than a highly organized pressure group. The Grange has a limited Washington staff—with only two lobbyists—and practically no research or economic policy. On the other hand, it has been successful in surviving as an organization because of its sociability. The Grange has members in Washington suburbs where the last farm has long since vanished. Yet partly because it tends to take a more moderate policy than the AFBF or the NFU, the Grange often does represent the centre of opinion in agricultural-policy issues.

The National Farmers' Organization. There is recurring interest amongst farmers in the idea of improving their lot by developing market power. The British National Farmers' Union encouraged its members to refrain from marketing stock in 1970 in order to put pressure on the government to raise subsidies. A much more interesting example occurred in the United States in the 1930s when the 'Farmers' Holiday' movement attempted to develop a strike weapon for farmers. The NFO was formed so that farmers could group together to secure, by bargaining together, a better deal from suppliers and processors than they could achieve individually. Farmers could help themselves more by improving their marketing position than by relying on politicians to raise their incomes.

Yet the NFO found it impossible to stay out of politics. This was partly because of the personality of the NFO's long-time President, Orin Lee Staley, a man with passionate views on agricultural politics. The NFO's drift into politics also reflects the radical tradition of the parts of the rural midwest from which its members come. But above all, the NFO found that it was pulled into politics by the law. The organization's plans to bargain collectively on behalf of farmers with the suppliers and customers ran into the problem of the anti-trust laws. In particular, the Supreme Court ruled that the law does not, as the NFO contends, provide special treatment for the farms and co-operatives. The liberal Supreme Court Justice Hugo Black argued that the relevant law, the Capper–Volstead Act, does not suggest Congressional desire 'to vest co-operatives with unrestricted power to restrain trade or to achieve monopoly by preying on independent producers, processors, or dealers intent on carrying on their business in their own legitimate way.' The attempt to modify these court rulings naturally involved the NFO in politics as part of the liberal farm bloc. Its political involvement broadened to defend farm-subsidy laws and attack 'agribusiness' and its Republican allies. Yet the non-political tradition in the NFO did not die. Indeed, in 1972 Orin Lee Staley came under severe criticism for being too political. He survived a strong challenge to his leadership that year, but subsequently fell from power.

The American Agriculture Movement. The tradition of the 'farm holiday' surfaced recently in a new movement, the American Agriculture Movement. The AAM was a consequence of farmers' frustrations over the rapid fall of prices in the mid-1970s and what they felt were breaches of campaign promises from Carter to raise subsidies to offset them. The AAM is not a formal organization, and to the embarrassment of police chiefs trying to deal with its demonstrations, has no formal leadership. Its members were advocates not only of withholding produce from markets but of militant demonstrations aimed at disrupting rush-hour traffic, especially in Washington DC. The AAM attracted much publicity by its tactics and galvanized farmers' organizations and Congress into action. Even the AFBF came out in favour of government action to stabilize prices, and faced with massive unrest amongst farmers whose votes he had courted so eagerly in 1976, Carter modified considerably his opposition to higher subsidies. Yet by 1979 the influence of the AAM had waned. The AAM was partly a victim of its own success, for as subsidies were raised, militancy declined. Moreover, antipathy to its militant tactics increased rapidly. The conventional farm organization and rural legislators found the Movement a considerable embarrassment, particularly as the key to raising subsidies, if necessary over the President's veto, lay in restoring close co-operation between urban and rural Democrats in Congress. The achievement of this co-operation produced a majority capable of overriding a veto from President Carter. The President promptly staged a re-retreat. Yet this co-operation between urban and rural Democrats was not eased by the AAM's disruptive tactics.

The Commodity Organizations

There are also dozens of commodity producers representing producers of a single commodity. Some of these, such as the Wheat Growers, are well-organized parts of the liberal farm bloc. Perhaps the most famous of the commodity organizations are the milk producers, who are large-scale contributors to political campaigns. Indeed, it is fairly certain that in 1972 the milk producers purchased an increase in the price of milk over the objection of the Secretary of Agriculture through a timely and large contribution to the Nixon 1972 campaign fund.

In general, however, commodity organizations suffer from their very nature as spokesmen for a certain kind of farmer only. In particular there are numerous potential conflicts within agriculture. Cattle producers tend to oppose higher prices for feed grains; feed-grain producers losing markets to sales of subsidized, surplus wheat. Politicians prefer to deal with national farm organizations which, representing producers of the full range of commodities, can help in the task of reconciling conflicting interests in agriculture in a comprehensive farm programme. However, the weakness of the general farm organizations has forced the farmers to turn to the commodity organizations for technical advice and help in formulating legislation.

The Character of Agricultural Interest Groups

Agricultural interest groups have a somewhat old-fashioned character. The wide-ranging conservatism of the AFBF, the semi-masonic character of the Grange, and the bitter disagreement between the agricultural interest groups on the fundamental principles of agricultural policy seem far removed from sophisticated policy-making. It is striking that the general farm organizations of the United States remain so unimpressive. After all, the dependence of the industry on government since the New Deal and its constant vulnerability to adverse market conditions would lead us to expect that farmers would develop cohesive, impressive organizations. The existing general farm organizations, of which the AFBF is by far the largest, seem ill suited to debates over farm-subsidy legislation. They seem even less well equipped to evaluate draft regulations from the Food and Drug Administration, the Environmental Protection Agency, and the ever growing number of federal agencies that affect modern, sophisticated farming.

There have been a few signs during the 1970s of the modernization of interest groups which we see so clearly in the business groups. In 1973 and 1976 the general farm groups—with the important exception of the AFBF—formed a coalition to lobby for the extension of the agricultural-subsidy laws. This attempt to create a united front was very much prompted by the recognition of how vulnerable subsidies were to attack from a Republican Administration when farmers constitute such a small proportion of the population. The creation of a more united farm bloc—spoilt of course by the absence of the largest of the farm organizations—was an important step in the creation of modern rural interest groups. Somewhat hesitantly, the AFBF has taken steps in the same direction by diluting the vehemence of its conservatism. For example, the AFBF has argued recently that the farm-subsidy laws should not be abolished, but that the subsidies should be fixed at very low levels. This marks a shift by the AFBF away from pure doctrine and towards a greater awareness of both political and agricultural reality. It may well be that as the smaller number of farmers is translated into reduced impact on Presidential and Congressional elections the farm groups will feel even more pressure to present a united, less ideological front.

So far, however, agricultural interest groups have demonstrated three features which we shall find surprisingly characteristic of American interest groups. First, all the groups together organize a low percentage of farmers in the United States. No more than 35 per cent of American farmers belong to any interest group, a density of membership far lower than the British National Farmers' Union enjoys. Second, American farmers are disunited. There are, as we have seen, not only numerous commodity groups but also competing and conflicting groups claiming to speak for all farmers. Third, the agricultural interest groups have not achieved that reputation for non-partisan, technical competence which successful British economic groups aim at. We shall now consider how far this is true of other economic groups, starting with unions.

Unions and Politics

It is widely believed that unions in the United States are not political. American unions are often contrasted in this respect with unions in Europe, which are often linked to Communist or Socialist parties. (It is rarer, for no good reason, to contrast American unions with Christian Democratic unions in Europe.) Yet, with one commendable exception,[1] political scientists have done little research on American unions, and though much energy has been spent constructing theories to explain why unions are a-political in the United States but not in Europe, few attempts have been made to check the accuracy of the claim.

It is indeed true that for much of their history, American unions shunned politics. The founder of the American Federation of Labor, Samuel Gompers, realized that one reason for the failure of many attempts to found enduring unions in the USA was that unions had involved themselves in radical—and therefore unpopular—politics. Gompers realized that union involvement in neither revolutionary nor party politics, which at that time was based primarily on appeals to ethnic or regional, rather than to class loyalties—was likely to help unions win members or acceptance. Moreover, Gompers saw little advantage in campaigning for the provision of state pensions and insurance schemes. After all, schemes controlled by unions would help to attract members. (It is amusing to note that Gompers, once a Marxist, justified his position by pointing out that after all the state was controlled by the bourgeoisie, and that the workers' savings should not be entrusted to it.[2]) Gompers was also insistent that unions should attempt to recruit only the most skilled members of the working class as the only section of it with the money, education, and discipline to sustain proper unionism. Craftsmen are rarely a group likely to support radical politics, and though perhaps more extreme than his Executive Council, Gompers was able to chart the course of the AFL until the Second World War. Only rarely, and then for reasons narrowly connected with unions' self interest did the AFL venture into the political arena.

It is easy to find unions which even now follow Gompers's approach to politics. Unions such as the Teamsters, the building trades unions, and the Maritime unions devote their political energies only to narrow objectives, though even these unions are more involved in politics than Gompers would have expected. The Teamsters endeavour politically to ensure that their close links with organized crime will not prove an embarrassment— or cause the government to take too close an interest in its enormous pension fund.[3] The Maritime unions have, with lavish campaign contributions, bought the friendship of members of the Congressional committees which decide on the level of subsidy and protection which American merchant shipping should enjoy. The building trade unions campaign assiduously, but only for legislation or contracts which will raise their members' wages. Yet the Gompers tradition does not explain the behaviour of all, or even of most, unions in the United States. There were always some unions associated with the AFL such as the International Ladies' Garment Workers' Union which were more political. There are even more unions which developed in a way very different to Gompers's craft unions.

The unionization of the unskilled came late to the United States. The AFL's lack of interest in the unskilled was not the only reason. Ethnic rivalries, regional differences, the lack of class consciousness, and the regular arrival of waves of mass immigration all made the task of the union organizers thankless. In the 1930s, however, the position changed. A minority of the AFL given powerful leadership by the President of the United Mineworkers, John L. Lewis, pressed hard for a drive to organize the unskilled workers. Some union leaders wanted to expand unions' base of support out of conviction. Others, including Lewis, were aware of the threat to their own unions which the existence of non-unionized, low-wage labour caused. The Committee for (later Congress of) Industrial Organizations, CIO, received little help from the AFL craft unions, naturally opposed to its strategy of organizing industries and not crafts. Indeed, it was this difference of approach which forced the CIO out of the AFL. The CIO did, however, have powerful help from the Congress. Senator Robert Wagner successfully sponsored a bill which bears his name, the Wagner Act, the first piece of federal labour legislation, which altered the balance of power in favour of unions and away from employers. A National Labor Relations Board was created and charged with the tasks of outlawing unfair labour practices on the part of employers (such as the use of company spies or dismissing workers for being in favour of a union), of giving workers the opportunity to vote in a secret ballot on whether they wished to belong to a union, and the powers to force employers to bargain in good faith with unions which demonstrated in ballots that they had the support of a majority of employees. Finally, to some extent prompted by the Wagner Act, the workers in mass-production industries, such as rubber and car factories and steel, displayed an enormous determination to create a union to represent them. After sit-ins made necessary by the impossibility of maintaining more conventional pickets outside the factories, and after enduring attacks by company police forces which in several instances resulted in the deaths of some strikers, unions such as the United Steelworkers and the United Auto Workers became established.

The CIO unions were heirs to a tradition very different from that of the AFL. In contrast to the moderation and legality the AFL had stressed, the CIO unions had emerged only because of their members' willingness to undertake militant, even illegal, action. Far from eschewing politics, the CIO unions had triumphed only because of the fact that friendly politicians occupied key positions. Had the Congress not passed the Wagner Act, or if Governors such as the Governor of Michigan, Frank Murphy, had been prepared to deploy the National Guard against the workers, the industrial unions might never have triumphed. Moreover, the CIO unions attracted to their cause and to positions within the unions idealists such as the Reuther brothers of the UAW. These were people with wide-ranging political and social concerns to whom the narrow outlook of the AFL was foreign.

In practice, however, the contrast between the AFL and the

CIO diminshed as time passed. During the 1940s, the AFL realized that the Wagner Act gave it, as well as the CIO, an opportunity; and AFL membership increased faster than the CIO's. The AFL appointed to its Presidency a man, George Meany, who had been a lobbyist for the AFL, and who, not surprisingly, was therefore much more committed to the involvement of unions in politics than most AFL officials were. In contrast, though the CIO remained more committed to politics in theory than the AFL, in practice it had done little to influence politics. Its tiny political action unit was almost disbanded in the years after the Second World War,[4] and the signs are that this decline in political involvement would have continued had it not been for an event which made clear the importance of politics to both wings of the union movement.

The employers and their friends in the Republican Party and amongst the Southern Democrats naturally disliked the boost the Wagner Act had given the unions. In the 1946 mid-term elections the Democrats suffered a stunning setback, and the Republicans organized both houses of Congress for the first time since 1930. The Republicans, led by Taft and Hartley in the Senate and House respectively, introduced a bill to shift the balance of power back towards employers; 'secondary' industrial action was to be outlawed, so that only those most immediately involved in a dispute could strike or picket; sympathy action became illegal. States were given the right to pass laws under Section 14(b) of the act which prohibited the closed shop. Partly because public opinion, incensed by the militant—and a-political—strikes Lewis had led in the coal industry without regard to the national interest during wartime or immediately thereafter, was strongly anti-union, Taft and Hartley were able to win enough support in Congress to override President Truman's veto of their bill. When comforting prophecies made by unions that those from industrial areas who had voted for the bill would be defeated at the next election proved groundless, both CIO and AFL unions throughout the country realized that not even the industrial strength of the unions was safe unless their involvement in politics increased.[5]

That lesson proved to be of enduring importance for American unions. It is often remarked in Britain that the American system of industrial relations is shaped by law. It is less often remarked that the administration of those laws is thoroughly permeated by politics. The membership of the National Labor Relations Board changes unusually rapidly for a regulatory agency in the USA, and so gives the President and the Senate the chance to change the complexion of the Board very rapidly. This opportunity has been taken. Scholars have seen a clear contrast between Boards appointed by Democratic Presidents, which are usually pro-union, and Boards appointed by Republicans, which are usually pro-management.[6] The Board has important discretion in interpreting the National Labor Relations Act, determining what exactly is, for example, secondary picketing. Yet this discretion is exercised within limits set by the courts, limits which have become narrower in recent years. This merely introduces another manner in which politics influence unions, however. The Supreme Court itself varies in its attitude towards unions, with Justices appointed by Republican Presidents by and large taking a more hostile attitude towards unions and a friendlier line with management than that of Democratic appointees, who are more likely to decide cases as unions wish. Thus even the industrial power of the unions is very seriously affected by political factors such as the attitudes to unions of the President, who nominates Justices, and the Senators, who confirm them. Whether they like it or not, unions since the Taft–Hartley Act have been obliged to take an interest in politics, and the serious setback its passage constituted for unions is a painful reminder that Gompers's strategy of keeping unions out of politics is now impossible.

Forms of Current Involvement in Politics

Until very recently, the political action departments of unions, and particularly that of the AFL-CIO, have been regarded as pace setters establishing levels of competence to which most other unions have merely aspired. The political strategies of American unions have consisted of three elements, the relative importance of which has varied. These elements are lobbying, electoral campaigning, and support for the Democratic Party.

Nearly every union in the United States employs staff in Washington who engage in lobbying. The number of lobbyists each union employs varies considerably, as do the issues on which unions lobby. Of course, many unions have lobbyists who work on issues only of immediate concern to their members. Others, such as the International Ladies' Garment Workers' Union, or the United Auto Workers, lobby on issues such as national health insurance which go far beyond the individual interests of the unions or the collective interests of the labour movement. Yet the world of the labour lobbyists is dominated by the American Federation of Labor-Congress of Industrial Organisations. The AFL-CIO has a comparatively large number of lobbyists, seven, who enjoy a reputation for unusually high competence. Although members of Congress pay regular compliments to the skill of the AFL-CIO lobbyists, it is rare that the exact nature of this skill is spelt out. In practice, the skills praised seem to amount to a thorough knowledge of the subject, and a thorough knowledge of both the people in Congress and the procedures of the institution. AFL-CIO lobbyists give valued advice on both the substance and the tactics of legislation. Surprisingly absent from the style of the AFL-CIO lobbyists is the use of explicit threats of campaign contributions to opponents, of the withdrawal of help in campaigns from the Committee on Political Education, COPE. The AFL-CIO lobbyists aim at building up trust. The influential *Congressional Quarterly* described the style of the chief lobbyist of the AFL-CIO, Ken Young, as follows:

He's very soft spoken, soft sell; he knows his facts. If you've got a question, he's got an answer for it. He doesn't threaten, he doesn't cajole, he doesn't plead. But he won't take 'no' for an answer . . . The AFL-CIO legislative department is marked by professionalism. They rarely come in heavy handed.[7]

Not all the individual unions behave in the same way; the *Congressional Quarterly* also commented that the light touch of the AFL-CIO was not used by all the individual unions. 'You get the legislative directors of the unions calling up and saying that they are withdrawing their money in the next election.' Moreover, a *Washington Post* series on unions and politics argued that 'Labor is not only competent and powerful. It is feared.'[8] Politicians are well aware that the COPE exists, and do not need explicit threats to be made aware of the electoral power of unions. Yet even friends of the AFL-CIO such as the former Representative from Illinois, Abner Mikva, have criticized the AFL-CIO for failing to use its electoral muscle sufficiently vigorously.[9] Some of the individual unions which are very

politically active, such as the UAW, echo the criticism, arguing
that the conciliatory attitude the AFL-CIO lobbyists adopt
squanders the considerable electoral strength the AFL-CIO
possess. The AFL-CIO lobbyists would argue that demands
that they throw their weight around more overestimate the
political power of labour, or of any other pressure group. As we
shall see, union membership, and therefore their greatest political strength, is limited to a few parts of the country. The
Representatives and Senators from the rural midwest, the south-
west, the south, and those—both Democrats and Republicans—
representing middle-class suburbs, have little to fear from the
electoral power of organized labour. A substantial proportion of
the members of the House and a majority in the Senate represent
areas where unions have little influence. If the AFL-CIO lobbyists are to create a majority in spite of this, they have to resort
to tactics which will win friends. In fact, the labour lobbyists
like to form coalitions. Ken Young has said: 'We do best when
we are part of a coalition.'[10] Partly for this reason, and partly
from conviction, the AFL-CIO lobbyists have long-standing,
almost institutionalized ties with other liberal pressure groups
such as the National Farmers' Union, the groups working for
civil-rights legislation, the coalition supporting national health
insurance, and the Americans for Democratic Action. The
AFL-CIO supports the major objectives of these groups, deploying its lobbyists to help them gain a majority in the Congress.
In return, the AFL-CIO hopes that it will receive help in its
campaign, so that, for example, the civil-rights groups will use
their special influence with the Black Caucus to win friends for
labour. The other response from the AFL-CIO to their minority
status is to rely on the persuasive powers of their lobbyists. The
persuasive powers of their lobbyists and the high quality of the
information at their disposal are not accidents. They are the
indispensable tools for winning the support of legislators whom
the AFL-CIO has power to coerce.

It is the machinery unions possess for intervening in election
campaigns that has been the most distinctive feature of political
action by unions, however. Most large organizations in the
United States are used to having someone—a lobbyist or a
lawyer—present their case to politicians. Few interests have as
much experience as unions in trying to determine which pol-

iticians are elected, and which are not. There are few permanent political organizations in the United States today which can compare with COPE. In the 1976 elections, COPE provided 120,000 volunteers, 20,000 telephones, and a computer system listing the names and addresses of 11 million union members to candidates whom it endorsed. A computer system was thought to be 'instrumental' in achieving 6 million new voter registrations. This system, which divides up the lists of union members and their families first by Congressional district and finally by street and block to help the canvassing of 'pro-labor' families is typical of the way in which COPE has pioneered the application of new technology to campaigning. Indeed, the COPE telephone banks, temporary telephone switchboards used by volunteers to canvas voters in a country where almost everyone has a telephone, are another example of the pioneering sophistication of COPE. COPE also organizes the distribution of large sums of money. Contributions made by COPE itself—perhaps $3 million in the 1976 elections—may be only just over a third of the total contributions to election campaigns by unions. However, COPE also co-ordinates the giving of campaign contributions by individual unions. COPE arranges meetings at which potential candidates can meet the political directors of unions who are often heavily influenced in their decision whether or not to make a contribution by the candidates's COPE rating—a percentage mark awarded on the basis of the candidate's votes on issues COPE feels to be important.[11] Richter has rightly drawn attention to the small percentage of unions' campaign contributions COPE supplies; however, he passes over the role of COPE in co-ordinating union contributions of admittedly tremendous sums.[12]

How much effect all this activity has is debated. Of course, the AFL-CIO believes that its support for candidates makes an important difference to their chances of success. Political scientists are more sceptical. The traditional view in the study of voting behaviour in the USA is that long-standing loyalty to a political party, party identification, determines the way in which most voters behave. According to this view, the candidates themselves, the issues they support, and the groups who campaign for the candidates make little difference. More recently, however, a rival school has argued that issues and individual candidates do indeed affect the outcome of elections.[13] The electorate is more aware of candidates' views than it was twenty-five years ago, more influenced by them, and less likely to stay loyal to one party; indeed, more voters than ever deny that they have any party allegiance, and call themselves independents. Yet both sides in the controversy agree that a majority of Americans retain a sense of party identification which affects considerably how they vote. As party identification is acquired from parents during childhood, there is little that unions can do to influence it. Thus, it is argued, voting behaviour is something which any pressure group is powerless to change in the majority of cases. Indeed, this general rule is supported by research conducted on unions themselves. Studies conducted in areas in which unions are strong—usually where the UAW operates, since it is amongst the most politically active of American unions—generally conclude that unions are of limited effectiveness in putting across their views on issues and candidates to members. In the pioneering survey of UAW members by Kornhauser *et al.*,[14] only 7 per cent of the membership described the union as the most important source of political information. In general, all the studies showed that there was no significant block of union voters willing to transfer its allegiance between candidates in line with the bidding of the union leaders.

Yet the studies do not show that the political work of unions is of as little consequence as has been suggested. Although only 16 per cent of UAW members studied cited the union as a source of political information, some signs of effective work by unions emerge. Thus all the studies find that union members support the political activities of unions, and two-thirds of UAW members surveyed by Sheppard and Masters claimed that they would be more likely to vote for a candidate if he or she was endorsed by the union. Above all, unions seem to be effective in counteracting the tendency for blue-collar workers to register and turn out to vote less frequently than the middle classes. Thus Sheppard and Masters reported of the UAW members they interviewed, 90 per cent had registered to vote, and 87 per cent actually voted, far higher figures than would be predicted from the socio-economic status of car workers.[15] In Connecticut, where the AFL-CIO is strong but does not dominate politics, it persuaded between 15,000 and 20,000 union families to register, enough to make the difference between success and failure for the candidates COPE supported.[16] Perhaps 6 million people were registered nationally by the AFL-CIO in 1976, an important aid to President Carter who was supported by COPE and by most workers.

Since 1972, a number of the most politically active and liberal of the unions, in particular the International Association of Machinists, the AFSCME, the UAW, the National Education Association, and the Oil, Chemical and Atomic Workers have banded together to form the Labor Coalition Clearing House. The Labor Coalition intervened to help a number of candidates for the Democratic Presidential nomination in 1976, all of whom were on the liberal wing of the party and who offered the unions, in exchange for their support, the inclusion on their slates of delegates to the Democratic convention people chosen by the unions. So far, however, the AFL-CIO itself has not participated actively in primary elections. Indeed, the issue of whether or not unions should participate actively in primaries raises the whole question of what the relationship ought to be between unions and the Democratic Party.

As we have noted, the early policy of the AFL was to avoid any involvement in party politics, eschewing both the formation of a Labor Party and links to either of the established parties, which of course in the nineteenth century were even less clearly based on class than at present. It is impossible to argue that this non-partisan policy has been maintained in practice, in spite of the claims to the contrary by leaders of the AFL-CIO, including the President of the organization from 1955 to 1979, George Meany. Officially the policy of the unions towards the parties was one of neutrality, honouring only Gompers's dictum that unions should reward their friends and punish their enemies. In practice, however, the unions came to work closely with the Democrats. Democrats were likely to support the unions on political issues linked to industrial relations; Democrats and unions were more likely, too, to agree on issues of a more general nature. Not surprisingly, therefore, the unions' lobbyists have their closest ties to Democrats, the Committee on Political Education gives its highest ratings and help in elections almost exclusively to Democrats, and relations between Democratic Presidents and the unions, though rarely tranquil, are much friendlier than with Republican Presidents.

Yet most unions have refused to commit themselves to the Democratic Party, and indeed relations between unions and the Democrats have been much stormier in the 1970s than at any time since the New Deal. At the heart of the matter was the development within the Democratic Party of new power blocks. Until the late 1960s, the unions were the only interest group in the Democratic Party which could expect to receive regular national attention. Of course, there were other interests which were represented in the party because of their local strength, such as the Texan oil concerns. However, only the unions were a nationally, effectively organized interest group, in practice, though not in theory, within the party. But throughout the 1960s and early 1970s, new issues produced new pressure groups within the Democratic Party. Blacks seeking civil rights, young people seeking peace in Vietnam, and women seeking equality turned to Democratic Party politics in the attempt to further their causes. The Peace Movement enjoyed the greatest success. Defeated in the attempt to win the nomination for Eugene McCarthy or Robert Kennedy (who was assassinated after his greatest success, in the Californian primary) the Peace Movement was able to secure a thorough revision of the practices of the Democratic Party and to succeed in 1972 in having the Democrats nominate a candidate, Senator George McGovern, who was an advocate of their cause.

Almost all these developments upset the unions. The reforms recommended to the Democratic Party (and adopted) by a Commission headed at first by Senator McGovern, then by Representative Fraser, had two main provisions. The first set quotas for each delegation to future Democratic conventions to achieve aims at securing minimum numbers of young people, blacks, and women to the Convention. Though most unions had been eager to help these groups achieve their policy goals, the unions resented the slight they imagined was implied in the failure to provide any corresponding quota for unions or blue-collar workers. The successful attempts to open up the process of selecting Democratic Party convention delegates made by the McGovern–Fraser Commission, which in practice often resulted in the adoption of primaries, were also seen by the unions as a reduction in their power. Most union leaders doubted their ability to persuade their members to turn out and vote in a *primary* election, let alone vote for a particular candidate; in contrast, when Democratic nominees had been chosen by the professional politicians, union leaders felt that the Party Convention, recognizing the importance of the unions, would choose a candidate acceptable to the unions. Moreover, often the *style* of many of the new groups—such as the Peace Movement— offended the often socially conservative union leaders. To the leaders of the AFL-CIO it all added up to a picture of a Democratic Party moving away from their influence and interests, and in 1972 the AFL-CIO took the unprecedented step of refusing to endorse the Democratic Party nominee for the Presidency, Senator McGovern, helping to ensure his massive defeat.

Events since 1972 have served to remind the unions that the Democratic Party is their best, but far from certain, hope. The Nixon and Ford Administrations certainly seemed to confirm that Republicans were unsympathetic to their objectives. Nixon himself turned out to be such a disappointment that by 1973 the AFL-CIO was campaigning for his impeachment. President Ford followed standard Republican policies. Spending measures passed by the overwhelmingly Democratic Congress to counteract the severe recession of 1973–6 were vetoed by the President; so too after confusion and delay, which increased the bitterness, was a measure designed to protect the industrial power of construction unions through a measure known as Common Situs Picketing. Not surprisingly, in 1976 the AFL-CIO worked whole-heartedly for the Democratic ticket headed by Governor Carter, although because of their policy of avoiding involvement in primaries, the unions, with the exception of those in the Labor Coalition, had enjoyed little influence in selecting the nominee. Indeed, in some ways the 1976 election typified the problems the unions have in operating in the new structure of the Democratic Party. On the one hand, the Republican candidates were totally unacceptable. On the other hand, the Democratic Party selecting its delegates predominantly in primaries produced a nominee about whom most union leaders were far from excited. To some extent this unhappy situation for the unions was a consequence of the AFL-CIO's failure to involve itself in primaries. Yet even those unions that did intervene under the banner of the Labor Coalition ended up in the somewhat bizarre position of supporting several similarly liberal but competing candidates.

Soon after the 1976 election it became obvious that the relationship between the unions and the Democrats had not returned to the smoothness of the period before the 1970s. Relations between the failing George Meany and President Carter were often stormy (unlike Meany's close relationship with that other Southern President, Lyndon Johnson). Though the Democrats did much to please the unions, such as reducing unemployment rather than inflation, their primary economic target, the unions suffered several serious setbacks. In particular, proposals from the unions for the passage of the Common Situs Picketing bill and a modest reform of the Labor Relations laws to prevent abuses on the part of employers were rejected by a Congress in which the Democrats, indeed the supposedly *liberal* Democrats, retained overwhelming strength. One inference which could be drawn from these setbacks was that the character of the Democratic Party, even the character of liberals within the party, had changed in a way which reduced the power of the unions. Elected by more suburban districts and by voters less tied to party loyalties, brought into politics by new issues such as environmental or consumer protection and the Vietnam War, even the liberal Democratic politician was out of tune with the socially reforming New Deal traditions of the majority of unions. Those with longer memories could suggest that, on the contrary, liberal Democrats had never been quite as loyal to the unions as the unions had been to liberal Democrats. In 1958–60, a Congress which again on paper looked very liberal had come perilously close to passing further legislation circumscribing the power of unions. Perhaps a reasonable conclusion to draw is that the unions have never been able to count on the instinctive loyalty of even liberal Democrats to their interests, and that their position in this respect has worsened. Certainly the unions seemed to find no comfortable posture in the 1980 primaries. Though ideological, and for a time tactical, considerations drew unions such as the IAM to Senator Kennedy, even liberal unions saw the disadvantages of offending an incumbent President. The UAW, for example, was conspicuously silent because it wanted President Carter to rescue Chrysler, the lame duck of the American car industry. Once more, unions found primaries hard to cope with.

The Purposes of Union Involvement in Politics

Many would admit that unions in the United States are extensively involved in politics, but would argue that, unlike their counterparts in countries which have a socialist tradition, American unions are concerned to defend only the most immediate of their interests. As we have seen, this belief does indeed reflect an important tradition—Gompersism—in American labour history. Yet as we have seen too, another tradition, the CIO tradition, is associated with a broader involvement of unions in politics than Gompers ever envisaged. Some of the sharpest arguments about unions, particularly amongst Democrats, focus on whether or not unions are a progressive, reforming group using their undoubted political muscle to help the disadvantaged, or whether, as their critics contend, they are merely a narrow, selfish, interest group.

Two points can scarcely be denied. First, unions differ considerably in the extent and purposes of their political involvement. Second, the political activities of the AFL-CIO itself extend far beyond union issues, though obviously including as well trade-union issues such as reform of the labour-relations laws. On both points, however, there are sharp divisions of opinion about where the balance lies. Thus at one end of the spectrum of union involvement in politics lie the United Auto Workers and American Federation of State County and Municipal Employees. Both unions take an extensive interest in politics, devote significant resources to it, and pursue numerous liberal causes which stretch far beyond the immediate concerns of their members. At the other extreme of the spectrum are the Teamsters and the craft unions (such as the Carpenters) which take little interest in any but the most immediate or instrumental of issues, and which have been prepared to support Republican, relatively conservative, candidates in return for narrow concessions on topics of interest to their unions or members alone.

It is hard to determine where the balance lies between these extremes. Most unions are probably closer to the UAW than to the craft unions in terms of the depth of political involvement. Moreover, as Richter has noted, individual unions are becoming more and more involved in politics, and their spending on politics has risen considerably. The limitation on campaign contributions (imposed by the 1974 Campaign Finances Act) to $5,000 per pressure group and the disillusion felt by the liberal unions over the political policies of George Meany in the early 1970s have encouraged this trend for individual unions to involve themselves in politics, rather than entrust political action to the AFL-CIO alone. Mention of the controversy caused within the AFL-CIO by topics such as Meany's refusal to endorse Senator McGovern in 1972 or his support for the involvement of the United States in the Vietnam War serve to remind us of the importance of general political rather than labour issues in the debates in the higher reaches of the labour movement. Of course, many factors, including personal rivalries and disagreements have played a part, but some of the climatic battles within the AFL-CIO, particularly those between Walter Reuther of the UAW and Meany have focused on issues such as Vietnam and the involvement of the AFL-CIO itself in programmes designed to foster the development of non-revolutionary trade unionism in Third World countries, particularly in Latin America. Both Meany's disagreements with Reuther and with the liberal unions which constituted the Labor Coalition Clearing House had a tendency to start with foreign policy but to broaden to a more general discussion of political rather than of union issues. The fact that political debates within the union movement have ranged over such a variety of topics is itself an argument against the idea that unions in the USA are interested only in industrial issues.

Yet the debates within the union movement also make it difficult to discuss dispassionately the extent to which the AFL-CIO helps the disadvantaged with its political strength. Thus when Reuther and the UAW broke with Meany, ostensibly on foreign-policy issues, Reuther soon broadened the debate by arguing the AFL-CIO was failing precisely in this respect. Reuther stated that he 'disagreed because the labor movement under his [Meany's] leadership is failing in the broad social responsibilities it has to the total community of America.'[17] Whether the AFL-CIO does *enough* to promote social reform is of course an evaluative question to be answered according to one's own beliefs as well as the facts. It ought to be un-controversial to assert that the AFL-CIO does a lot on issues of concern to society in general, and not just the unions or their members.

A variety of evidence points to the conclusion that the political activities of the AFL-CIO are not primarily, let alone exclusively, focused on what one would define as pure labour issues. Inter-views with Representatives and Senators, the published reports of the AFL-CIO lobbyists, and perhaps most significant of all, the scales used by the Committee on Political Education to evaluate legislators, all suggest that union issues play a small part in the political work of the AFL-CIO. One Representative told the author: 'I can't remember the last time they contacted me on a pure labour issue. Was it 14(b) of Taft Hartley in 1965? No, there was one thing last year. But it's civil rights, housing, health insurance.' Between 1970 and 1976 only thirty out of ninety-nine issues used by COPE to evaluate the voting record of Senators could be defined as issues concerning labour relations or unions. The pattern in evaluating Representatives was much the same. Only thirty out of ninety-two issues used to evaluate Representatives since 1970 were pure labour or union issues. This is not to argue that unions are an altruistic movement devoting their strength to helping others. Unions do in fact devote considerable attention to issues which will not primarily and immediately benefit their members. About 12 per cent of the issues handled by COPE and the AFL-CIO lobbyists were issues such as renewal of the Voting Rights Act, a measure targeted on the South where unions are weak. The bulk of the unions' efforts, however, goes into issues such as National Health Insurance, measures to secure full employment, and public-housing projects which benefit both unions and working but non-unionized Americans as well. Of course union members would gain from the implementation of national health in-surance or full employment in the United States. Many people without the benefit of occupational health-insurance schemes (which most unions negotiate) would gain even more from national health insurance; groups more marginal to the economy—such as blacks—with high rates of unemployment gain even more from full employment than do most union members. This combination of interest, though, between the unions and the less advantaged sectors of American society is the surest ground for assuming that they will continue to play a liberal role in politics.

The second factor which will bind the unions to politics is one we encountered in explaining the growth of the involvement of American unions in politics since the Second World War. The American system of industrial relations is one based on law but suffused with politics. Tens of thousands of cases touching on the rights of unions in general as well as determining the success or failure of unions in particular plants work their way through labour courts, and often on appeal through the federal courts to the highest court of all, the Supreme Court. It is vital for the unions to prevent either the basic labour laws being changed in a direction which would disadvantage them, or the laws being interpreted in a manner which would reduce their power. The unions cannot be indifferent to the composition of Congress, or who occupies the White House and appoints those who interpret and enforce the labour laws. In practice, it is Democratic appointees who are likely to sympathize with the unions.

It is often imagined that the unions have created a position for themselves on labour law issues which is totally safe, which- ever party controls the Presidency. Indeed, the unions are often cited as a classic example of clientelism. Both the committees of Congress most concerned with labour issues, the Department of Labor and the regulatory commission, the National Labor Relations Board, are said to be very sympathetic to the unions. The argument has some merits. The Representatives and Senators on the Education and Labor Committee and the Labor and Public Welfare (now Labor and Human Resources) Committee are by and large sympathetic to unions. In the House of Representatives, the unions secure a sympathetic hearing from the majority party; only liberal pro-labour Rep- resentatives are put on the Education and Labor Committee by the Democrats. In the Senate, the unions do even better as several of the Republican Senators on Labor and Human Resources are on good terms with the unions.

Yet in the executive agencies the picture is less clear, and it should be noted that even in Congress, the Republican minority on the House committee have a strongly anti-union reputation.

It runs very much against the grain for Republicans, except the mavericks such as Javits, to support unions against management. For this reason, Republican administrations have found it difficult to find people available to serve as political appointees in the Department of Labor who can meet the tests of being able to work with the unions and of being loyal party members. Eisenhower appointed an official of the Plumbers' Union as his Secretary of Labor, but the Secretary, Durkin, soon resigned to be succeeded by a Vice-President of Bloomingdale's, the large New York department store. President Nixon was unable to keep any Labor Secretary for very long, and ended up with an academic expert on unions who was probably a Democrat; in any case, Nixon's last Secretary of Labor, John Dunlop, was virtually forced to resign by President Ford, who destroyed the Secretary's credibility when he vetoed a bill on common situs picketing which Dunlop had supported. People who are sympathetic to unions may well be suited to the Department of Labor; they are rarely suited to Republican administrations. It is instructive to note that Dunlop's fall was occasioned by a serious challenge to President Ford from Governor Reagan for the Republican Party nomination. In Republican primaries, sympathy for unions is a decided disadvantage. Though Republicans in recent years—particularly President Nixon and Vice-President Ford—have tried to win blue-collar votes by appealing to the supposedly conservative attitudes of workers on social and foreign policy issues, the attempts by the Nixon and Ford administrations to develop close links with any but the most corrupt of unions, such as Teamsters, met with very short-term success.

The Unions and Politics

In many respects, unions have led the rest of the economic interest groups in developing political skills and resources. No other economic group has an electoral action organization to compare with COPE: few interest groups, if any, have lobbyists as respected as the AFL-CIO's. Yet the value of this machinery should not be overestimated. Whenever labour fights alone—as on labour law reform or common situs picketing—it loses. Even when unions have friends—as on national health insurance—success is not assured. Lobbyists can cajole, but cannot control;

voting behaviour in the USA is shaped by deeper, stronger forces than the efforts of union officials to deliver their members' votes. Indeed, in many respects the involvement of unions in politics in the USA is a mark of weakness, not strength. If unions were not so weak industrially, representing only 21 per cent of the workforce, if they did not have to operate within the framework of industrial relations laws which have been shaped contrary to the wishes of the unions and which curtail their power, and if greater class-consciousness in the USA had produced a social-democratic party comparable to those of northern Europe, then unions would have had less need to involve themselves in politics so directly. In Sweden, and at times in Britain, unions have been seen by Government as so important that it is obvious that they must be conciliated on many issues nominally in the hands of politicians. In northern Europe social-democratic parties have gained power and introduced all of the welfare state measures for which American unions are still striving. Even in the realm of industrial relations, were the unions less active politically, the law would be written and administered in a manner which would weaken the power of unions even further. It is easy, but fallacious, to assume that the greatest political effort is expended by those who possess the most resources and the most power to begin with. American unions are organizations which are politically active not because they are in a strong position but because they are in a weak position.

Unions and the Interest-Group System

Unions are the most developed politically of economic interest groups in the United States. However, unions also illustrate— like the agricultural interest groups—the political weakness rather than the strength of economic groups in the United States. In particular, the unions suffer from limited member- ship, disunity and questionable status. The proportion of the American workforce organized by unions (21 per cent) is falling. Three of the largest unions—the Teamsters, the National Education Association, and the United Auto Workers—are not affiliated to the AFL-CIO. Nor is the United Mine Workers. Divisions between American unions, with the UAW on the left and the Teamsters on the right, are even deeper than between

British unions. Moreover, unions suffer from two blows to their standing with politicians—the enmity of conservative politicians and the deserved reputation of some unions, such as the Teamsters, for gangsterism and corruption. Even the extensive and impressive political efforts of the AFL-CIO do not completely overcome these difficulties. We turn next to the role that business has played in American politics.

4

Business and Politics

Marxist scholars have long contended that the state exists to serve the interests of capitalists, that government is, in the words of Marx and Engels, the executive committee of the bourgeoisie.[1] More recent Marxist scholarship has been concerned to argue that the subordination of the political system to the interests of the economic system is not total. Producing something of a convergence of Marxist and non-Marxist scholarship, traditional political scientists are less wont than they used to be to argue that the relationship between business and government is no different to the relationship between government and any other interest group. There has been a growing awareness of how the dictates of the economic system and circumstances limit the options available to governments. Thus Charles Lindblom, an eminent political scientist scarcely thought of as a radical, has argued[2] that business is not just another interest group trying to influence government. Because in societies like the USA businessmen have been entrusted with organizing the wealth-creating activities of society, they are an equal partner with which government must negotiate. Business, in brief, holds a 'privileged position'. Governments in market economies such as the United States must induce rather than command business to perform in promoting employment and economic growth. Any government official in a market society must recognize the need to make concessions to business. When a government official asks himself whether business needs a tax deduction he knows he is asking a question about the welfare of the whole society and not merely about a favour to a segment of that population which is what is typically at stake when he asks himself should he respond to an interest group.

Any government official who understands the requirements of his position and the responsibilities that market-oriented systems throw on businessmen will therefore grant them a privileged position . . . *He does not have to be bribed, duped or pressured to do so.* Nor does he have to be an uncritical admirer of businessmen to do so. He simply understands, as is plain to see, that public affairs in a market oriented society are in the hands of two groups of leaders, government and business, and that to make the system work, government leadership must often defer to business leadership.[3]

There are a number of difficulties with the central part of Lindblom's argument. First, as Lindblom acknowledges, there are occasions when governments defy the wishes of businessmen. Not all governments, or perhaps any government all the time, gives businessmen what they want. Second, whereas Lindblom would argue that such defiance will exact an economic penalty, it is clear that businessmen do not always know their own best interest as well as government does. Had businessmen had their way the New Deal would never have happened, and Landon would have been elected President in 1936. Yet Roosevelt, as instigator of the New Deal, is often thought of today as the saviour of American capitalism. Lindblom argues that one reason for the political success of businessmen is that

businessmen do nothing more than persuade. They simply acquaint government officials with the facts. But prophecies of some kinds tend to be self-fulfilling. If spokesmen for businessmen predict that investment will lag without tax relief, it is only one short step to corporate decisions that put off investment until tax relief is granted.[4]

In contrast, one can argue that businessmen are, like the famed shepherd boy in the fable, always crying wolf. Had the protestations of businessmen been accepted at face value, very few social reforms would have been adopted, as Charles Dickens pointed out in *Hard Times*.

Surely there was never such fragile china-ware as that of which the manufacturers of Coketown were made. Handle them ever so lightly and they fell to pieces with such ease that you might suspect them of having been flawed before. They were ruined when they were required to send labouring children to school; they were ruined when inspectors considered it doubtful whether they were quite justified in chopping people up with their machinery; they were utterly undone when it was hinted that perhaps they need not always make quite so much smoke . . . Whenever a Coketowner felt he was ill-used— that is, whenever he was not left entirely alone, and it was proposed to hold him accountable for any of his acts—he was sure to come out with the awful menace that he would 'sooner pitch his property into the Atlantic.' This had terrified the Home Secretary within an inch of his life on several occasions.[5]

It may well be that businessmen everywhere complain about government interference with the monotonous regularity that farmers complain about the weather. However, the degree to which businessmen are genuinely concerned about government policies varies quite considerably from period to period. In this chapter we shall see that the relationship between business and politics in the United States has gone through three stages in the postwar period. The first of these was a period of complacent inactivity which ended in the early 1960s; the second a period of covert, and not particularly effective, involvement which ended around 1974; and finally, a more open and successful involvement deploying many of the traditional techniques of pluralist politics.

The Era of Complacency

Until recently, American businessmen felt little need to engage actively in politics. As late as 1961, the giant American-based multinational International Telephone and Telegraph (ITT) did not maintain a Washington office. When ITT did open such an office a redoubtable lady, Dita Beard, was able to rise from secretary to lobbyist in a matter of weeks because so few people in the company knew anything of how to win in Washington. 'Within a very short time I realised that none of them [Executives] knew the name of the game in Washington. They had no political representation. They were babes in arms.'[6]

A more systematic analysis of the role of business in politics at this time was made by Bauer, Pool, and Dexter in their massive study, *American Business and Public Policy*.[7] Their study showed that most business lobbyists were under-financed, ill informed, and ineffective. Most firms had not even communicated with Congress within the last two years. Thus only 37 out of 166 large firms and 68 out of 404 medium-sized firms they surveyed had communicated with Congress in the previous two years.[8] Nor was this inactivity by individual firms compensated for by trade associations which were often deeply divided on issues. 'When we look at a typical lobby we find that its opportunities for manoeuvre are sharply limited, its staff mediocre and its typical problem not the influencing of Congressional votes but the finding of clients and contributors to enable it to survive at all.'[9] Not surprisingly, 'The role of trade association executives is not highly regarded by American business.' Neither did these lobbyists have a high standing with Congressmen. Because of their powerlessness and dependence on sympathetic legislators, 'the lobbyist becomes in effect a service bureau for those Congressmen already agreeing with him rather than an agent of direct persuasion.'[10]

Here and there Bauer, Pool, and Dexter produce pieces of evidence to suggest that their unflattering portrait of the political skills of American business does not accurately reflect the potential of giant companies. Thus Bauer *et al.* remark of Du Pont; 'Of course Du Pont is continually involved in relationships with the United States government, but like most big corporations it tends to deal directly with the relevant government agency than requesting Congressional aid' (p. 267). Later in the study the authors note the competence and knowledge which Standard Oil could deploy in policy debates (pp. 347–8) and that Westinghouse at one stage did unleash a 'quite massive barrage' of pressure on Congress (p. 358). Bauer *et al.* also report with probably unwise denigration, 'we were told, with dark hints but never with substantial fact, of supposed pressure by the Big Five of the oil industry on 'small independents' to prevent their taking a firm restrictionist stand' (p. 363). They do not explain how these comments are consistent with their general findings based on survey material. Perhaps the explanation is that the examples of political action on the part of giant corporations, which they mention in passing, refer to a statistically insignificant number of cases of very large firms in some unusual industries such as the oil industry.

It would be wrong, therefore, to suggest that American business was altogether politically naïve in the 1950s. Defence contractors were aware that it was as well to supplement patriotism and technical skill with political influence if a contract was to be won.[11] The whole structure of the oil industry was dependent on political decisions such as restriction on the amount of oil which could be imported and on enabling oil companies to charge prices above the world market rate. The oil companies also enjoyed the benefits of an oil-depletion allowance which authorized them to claim a tax concession of 27.5 per cent beyond[12] that allowed to ordinary corporations. None the less, as the survey by Bauer, Pool and Dexter indicated, politics was of little relevance to most companies—even to large companies—and as we saw ITT, even a giant multinational, could be surprisingly naïve politically as late as 1961.

Of course, as radicals argued, this political inactivity on the part of business was eminently comprehensible in the context of American politics in the late 1950s. President Eisenhower's first Cabinet contained eight millionaires and one of them, Defense Secretary Charles Wilson, was the famed author of the saying 'What is good for the United States is good for General Motors and vice versa.' As sociologists such as C. Wright Mills[13] and G. William Domhoff[14] pointed out, people at the top of different walks of life in the United States—business, politics, civil service, and the military—shared a common background and education. The population at large showed considerable confidence in businessmen and what was often called the free-enterprise system. Politicians had little incentive, therefore, to take an anti-business line. Indeed, opponents or critics of the free-enterprise system were scarcely likely to flourish in the decade of McCarthyism unless—like Kefauver with his criticisms of the drug industry—such criticisms could be focused on narrow but dramatic abuses. Business had little reason to pay much attention to politics in the 1950s unless—as in the oil and defence industries—the nature of their work brought them into close contact with government. In general, the political climate was so favourable to business that political mobilization would have been wasteful.

Not surprisingly, the absence of political challenges to business in general produced particularly weak general business interest groups. Furthermore, the issues which did arise—such as the lowering of tariff rates studied by Bauer, Pool, and Dexter were likely to affect industries and corporations differentially so that general business interest groups would be handicapped by a divided membership. Of course, general business interest groups did exist.

The NAM and the Chamber of Commerce

The National Association of Manufacturers had been founded in 1893 and the Chamber of Commerce in 1912 at the prompting of President Taft. Neither was treated with much respect in Washington. Indeed, in an article published in 1953, Richard Gable addressed a popular question when he asked 'NAM, Influential Lobby or Kiss of Death?'[15] The answer was more likely the latter. Membership of NAM had peaked at 22,000 during the Korean War and thereafter declined to 13,000 by the early 1970s.[16] Though the saying was that the NAM spoke for Pittsburgh business, the Chamber of Commerce for Main Street business, more manufacturing firms belonged to the Chamber than to the NAM. However, the similarities between the business-lobby groups were more significant than the differences. Most legislators were aware of what the Chamber of Commerce and the NAM were against—higher taxes on businessmen, labour unions, and welfare—but few knew what they favoured. Somewhat later than the period we are concerned with, Henry Reuss (D. Wisc.) described the Chamber as 'unbelievably negative and backward looking' (1969).[17] His comments were applicable to the whole history of the Chamber in the postwar period until 1974. The plaque in the office of the Director of the NAM used to read: 'Where we stand in the Effort to Save the Free Enterprise System' and then listed a series of highly ideological policy positions.[18] In the early 1960s the Chamber of Commerce devoted itself to running courses for businessmen on such critical choices facing policy makers as 'Freedom versus Communism'.[19] An oil-company executive in Houston echoed the spirit of such campaigns when he said: 'All we want to do is to inform our people [employees]. . . . We don't want to make conservatives out of them! Nosiree! We want them to take a look at the Soviet system and compare it with our free enterprise.'[20] This was hardly being engaged in practical politics. Bauer, Pool, and Dexter's low estimate of the effectiveness of the NAM and the Chamber of Commerce on practical issues was surely justified. In the absence of challenges to the collective interests of business, interest groups for the collective defence of business interests did not flourish.

It followed from this that if businessmen were confronted with a significant challenge to their mutual interests, it was more likely that stronger organizations would emerge to defend these collective interests.

The Growth of Political Involvement

Such a challenge was mysteriously conjured up in the late 1950s and early 1960s. Businessmen, not for the last time, were seriously disconcerted by liberal Democratic triumphs, on this occasion in the 1958 midterm elections, and, again not for the last time,

seriously overestimated the threat this posed to corporations.
(In the event the 1958–60 Congress was to pass labour legislation, the Landrum Griffin Act, closer to the wishes of corporations than to those of unions, the supposed friends of the liberal
Democrats.) The election of John Kennedy, a liberal-moderate
Democrat, in 1960 seems to have occasioned businessmen some
further concern. In retrospect, it is hard to see why businessmen
should have been at all disturbed by the Kennedy Administration. There was, of course, a confrontation between Kennedy
and the steel corporations when these corporations, having
benefited from Kennedy's pressure on the Steelworkers' Union
to moderate a wage claim immoderately increased prices themselves. Kennedy certainly did play 'hardball' as Americans say,
by using all the techniques at his disposal to put that pressure
on the steel corporations. Apart from plans to switch government
purchases to those steel companies that had not increased
prices, FBI agents were dispatched on night-time searches to
find evidence of a conspiracy to raise prices in breach of the
anti-trust acts. Moreover, to many businessmen, any government intervention in pricing decisions was intolerable. The
slow acceptance of a Keynesian economic policy by the
Kennedy Administration may also have startled a few businessmen, though the form of the stimulus to the economy that
Kennedy used—a tax cut, not increased government
expenditure—was the most acceptable to the business community. Perhaps all that disturbed businessmen was the more
liberal character of the Administration compared with that of
its predecessor. Of course, there were businessmen, such as the
Secretary of the Treasury, Dillon, and the Defense Secretary,
MacNamara, in the Kennedy Administration. But there were
also those such as J. K. Galbraith and Arthur Schlesinger (Jr.)
whom business magazines perversely identified as enemies.[21]
There is, too, the same instinctive identification between
businessmen and a Republican Administration—and conversely
suspicion of a Democratic one—that there is amongst British
businessmen and the Conservatives. In an interesting slip while
explaining how her work was purely with Congress, the ITT
lobbyist, Dita Beard, was to tell a Senate Committee, 'I haven't
been in the White House once in the three years *we* have been in
office',[22] by which she meant the Republicans.

If none of these seems a good reason for businessmen to be concerned about the Kennedy Administration, one returns to the ease with which the business community can be frightened politically. On taking office after the assassination of President Kennedy, Lyndon Johnson arranged a meeting with prominent businessmen at which he quoted to them the opinion of the veteran Speaker of the House, Sam Rayburn. 'Businessmen are the most scared people in Washington. If he can't scare himself enough a businessman will hire a lawyer or a public relations man to keep him scared.'

Whatever the reason, the early 1960s did see a concerted effort to involve businessmen in politics. Representatives of prominent firms such as Ford's berated meetings of businessmen about the absurdity of 'businessmen who spend their leisure hours indignantly berating the actions of government [but] are content when they go to work to take their place in a management structure which concerns itself 99 per cent with non-governmental factors and at best 1 per cent with the impact of business on government.'[23] In the early 1960s the Chamber of Commerce was sending out numerous primers on how to become involved in politics—7,000 a month before the 1960 election. President Eisenhower emerged from retirement in 1962 to urge businessmen to rally to the Republican Party. Republicans were the party of business, and he was 'proud of the label'. He added: 'Businessmen now have to do a little waking up. Businessmen can no longer be sure that there are well designed and well observed limits beyond which government will not go. If businessmen do not realise the need, they are not going to have a prosperous business in the long run.'[24] In August 1963 a group of businessmen from non-Wall Street firms formed the Business Industry Political Action Committee, BIPAC. Its objective was to solicit campaign contributions from businessmen and to channel them to conservative politicians, thereby offsetting the influence of the AFL-CIO's Committee on Political Education. The formation of BIPAC was supported by the NAM which commented that 'Federal over regulation, over investigation and over control' was a barrier to economic growth.[25]

The formation of BIPAC was not of as much significance as might have been supposed. A number of changes were necessary before the political-action committees would mushroom in the

1970s. One of these changes was in the law. Another was to close off easier ways of influencing politicians. The movement to involve businessmen directly in politics foundered on their unwillingness to ring doorbells or to fill envelopes with campaign literature. Their companies found other ways to intervene in politics. The practice of companies making donations to the campaigns of politicians became very common in spite of its prohibition by 18 US Code 610.

It shall be unlawful for any corporation whatever to make a contribution or expenditure in connection with any election at which Presidential and Vice Presidential electors are to be voted for, or in connection with any primary election or political convention or caucus held to select candidates for any of the foregoing offices.

A further clause extended the prohibition to candidates for Congress. Both sections of the law were to be breached almost as often as parking regulations.

The technique used to circumvent 18 US Code 610 was to pretend that the money came from businessmen, not from corporations. Both President Kennedy and President Johnson had a 'President's Club' which raised campaign funds from businessmen. In return, members received prompt attention to any problems they encountered with the Federal government. Illegal campaign contributions became more common during the Nixon Presidency, however. We owe it to the Select Committee on Campaign Practices (the Ervin Watergate Committee) that there has been such good documentation of the use of these techniques. Companies passed money to campaigns either through trusted employees or through foreign subsidiaries, a process known as 'laundering' the funds. The first technique was favoured by the American Shipbuilding Corporation, the latter by Gulf Oil and the Minnesota Mining and Manufacturing Corporation. 'I was informed by him [the Company Secretary] that I had a bonus of $5,000 and that I was to make out a cheque for $3,000 to a Committee to Re-Elect the President.' Executives planning such practices, as in this example, knew of their illegality.[26]

One of the standard problems in criminology is how far crime statistics reflect the level of illegal activity. Not all illegal acts are detected; not all crimes are solved. The problem which confronts us is the extent to which the successful investigations by the Watergate Special Prosecutors and the Securities and Exchange Commission unmasked illegal campaign contributions. Herbert Alexander, in his study of the financing of the 1972 election, has concluded that illegal corporate campaign contributions to the Nixon campaign amounted to $1,350,000 of which one-third was returned. Another question which we might wish to answer is the proportion of corporations engaged in making illegal campaign contributions. As not all corporations running illegal political action programmes were detected by the prosecutors, the total is hard to assess. Business sources have estimated, however, that at least one-third of the top Fortune 500—the largest and most prestigious of the American corporations—made systematic, but illegal, campaign contributions.[27] Amongst some of the more dramatic revelations were that the Northrop Aircraft corporation had kept a $30 million secret political fund,[28] that Gulf Oil had run a $10 million secret fund,[29] while Phillips Petroleum gave away $2.8 million illegally. The Minnesota Mining and Manufacturing Company admitted that between 1963 and 1969, $634,000 had been laundered through payments supposedly to foreign legal counsel, but in fact to politicians selected by the chief executive officer.[30]

The system of illegal contributions which operated so extensively in the 1960s had three major characteristics. First, the amounts dispensed to politicians were relatively small. Thus most of the payments from the Minnesota Mining and Manufacturing Company were for merely hundreds of dollars and the largest single payment was for $15,000. Second, the payments to politicians were distributed over a reasonably wide part of the political spectrum, from centre-left to centre-right, and were regarded as a normal part of the political process. Recipients included Richard Nixon, Hubert Humphrey, and the once powerful chairman of the House Ways and Means Committee, Wilbur Mills. Senator Hugh Scott, Republican leader in the Senate, regarded the payments as so normal that he found it almost impossible to believe that they would ever end. Scott received $10,000 directly from Gulf Oil; an additional $2,000 was routed to him via his law firm. After the illegal payments to the Nixon campaign by Gulf had been discovered, Gulf's lobbyist, Wild, told Scott that all other illegal payments by Gulf would have to stop too. 'Wild told the Senator that he could no longer provide the money, but the Senator seemed at a loss to understand why.'[31] Third, the illegal payments were not usually regarded as bribes related to specific decisions—though as we shall see that was not unknown—but were intended to secure goodwill and access. Thus the system by no means represented the total domination of politicians by business. The point was well put by Mr Atkins of Ashland Oil. Asked by the Senate Watergate Committee Counsel, 'Can you think of any way that your corporation was distinctively benefited by its contribution?' Mr Atkins replied: 'I am afraid that I cannot. It is an unfortunate statement to make on behalf of our share-holders but I can see no way we were benefited . . . its intention was to give us a means of access to present our point of view to the executive branch of the Government.'[32] Mr Atkins was explaining payments to CREEP; payments to Congressmen and Senators were made on the same basis.

Our interest in the illegal payments made by so many of the giant corporations in the United States should not blind us to the more normal political pressures exerted by them. The illegal payments seem to have been made systematically by most corporations from about 1961 onwards and represented the increased political activity on the part of business we have already noted. There were, however, normal or honest attempts to persuade politicians from an increasing number of corporation lobbyists. Very frequently, corporations followed a strategy of combining judiciously both legal and illegal efforts to influence politicians. In both cases of legal and illegal tactics the tendency in the 1960s was for corporations to 'go it alone'. As Epstein noted, by 1969 corporations were no longer unwilling to 'ac-knowledge that they have specific political interests which they seek to further by active political participation'. Fifty-three per cent of firms with more than 5,000 employees, 35 per cent of medium-sized firms (499–5,000 employees) and 20 per cent of small firms (1–500 employees) monitored legislation continu-ously. Ninety per cent of the firms surveyed had communicated with state or federal legislators on an issue of concern to the corporation in the previous two years, though only 20 per cent had done so frequently.[33]

ITT Works the System

The corporation whose involvement in politics in the late 1960s and early 1970s was investigated the most thoroughly was the International Telephone and Telegraph corporation. ITT faced two major problems which required a political solution. First, as the most conspicuous of the new conglomerates which had built up their size by merging with firms in apparently unrelated industries, ITT was a natural target for trust-busters, including the traditionally independent and vigorous Anti-Trust Division of the Justice Department. Second, ITT owned the telephone system in Chile which the constitutionally elected President of Chile, Salvador Allende Grossens, was threatening to nationalize without compensation. ITT stood to lose an investment valued at $1,500 million.

Somewhat surprisingly, the man appointed to head the Anti-Trust Division of the Justice Department by Nixon, Richard McClaren, was a lawyer with very strong views on the anti-trust laws. In particular, contrary to conventional wisdom subscribed to by many including Solicitor General Griswold (a hold-over from the Johnson Administration), McClaren believed that no fresh legislation was required to enable the Justice Department to obtain court orders against conglomerates as monopolies. Because McClaren's view was unconventional, it was likely that a Supreme Court ruling would be needed to substantiate his view, and McClaren's main objective became to obtain such a decision. Three ITT mergers, one with Grinell, one with the Canteen catering company, and the other with the Hartford Insurance Company, seemed to provide suitable opportunities for McClaren to test his view of the law. McClaren, therefore, brought an action against ITT, and after losing—as he had anticipated—in the lower courts, he moved the case to the Supreme Court. A few days before the cases were due to go before the Supreme Court, they were withdrawn somewhat mysteriously after a negotiated settlement with ITT which did nothing to establish the precedent that McClaren wanted. McClaren left the Anti-Trust Division to take up a federal judgeship, a political appointment. Jack Anderson, the syndicated columnist, obtained and published memoranda from the ITT lobbyist, Dita Beard, which seemed to link the decision to an offer by ITT to provide substantial funds towards the cost of meeting the President's wish to hold the Republican Party Convention of 1972 in San Diego. Beard referred to the money as 'our noble commitment'.[34]

The main concern of the Senate Judiciary Committee was to discover whether the payment offered by ITT was indeed the reason for the failure to take the case to the Supreme Court. The hearings were to uncover much, however, on the ways in which ITT tried to influence government decisions. In actual fact, there is little complicated to describe. ITT worked determinedly on the top officials of the Executive branch of government, including the White House staff. The strategy was summarized in a memorandum the ITT Vice-President, Ireland, addressed to the company President, Geneen, calling 'in your own apt phrase from an earlier conversation . . . [for a strategy] of "inexorable pressure" right up and through the moment the deed [merging with Hartford Insurance] is officially consumated.' ITT secured an enormous number of meetings with officials of an Administration not in general known for its openness. Between 1969 and early 1971, Geneen saw seventeen Cabinet Secretaries or members of the White House staff in an attempt to persuade the Administration not to block acquisition of further companies by ITT. Geneen met the Commerce Secretary, Stans, Attorney General Mitchell (who had entrusted the anti-trust question to Deputy Attorney General Kleindienst because of a conflict of interest) and John Ehrlichman, the man closest to Nixon in the White House. The ITT Vice-President, Gerrity, met McClaren himself and other White House staff such as Herb Klein and Harry Dent. At crucial moments during the Justice Department's debate about how to handle the case, Geneen met the President's Chief Economic Adviser, the Secretary of the Treasury, and Peter Flanigan and Peter Peterson, members of the White House staff specializing in economic affairs. In brief, the officers of ITT had numerous opportunities to lobby the highest officials of the Administration and enjoyed access to decision makers not exceeded by any other Washington lobby.

What part was played by the less salubrious offer of money for the Republican Convention? Both ITT and the Administration denied any connection. Both, however, had good reason to do so. Apart from any general embarrassment, the Senate

Judiciary Committee's enquiry was linked to hearings on the nomination of Kleindienst to succeed Mitchell as Attorney General. As Kleindienst was responsible for the ITT case (because of Mitchell's conflict of interest in the case,) any confirmation that the State Department had 'gone soft' on ITT because of the offer of $400,000 for the Republican Convention would have resulted in rejection of Kleidienst's nomination by the Senate. Kleindienst's denial that the payment was linked to the decision on the ITT case is further weakened by the fact that he committed perjury in his testimony to the Senate Judiciary Committee. The position was put clearly by the House Judiciary Committee in its report recommending impeachment of Nixon.

During the hearings before the Senate Committee on the Judiciary on Richard Kleindienst's nomination to be Attorney General of the United States Kleindienst and former Attorney General Mitchell gave false testimony regarding the President's involvement in the case. Clearly Kleindienst and Mitchell were protecting the President. Kleindienst testified he had not received direct direction from the White House about ITT cases. In fact on April 19, 1971, the President had ordered Kleindienst to drop an appeal in the ITT case and that anti-trust chief McClaren be sacked if this was not done.[35]

This does not take us much further, however. The order from Nixon referred to was subsequently rescinded on advice from Mitchell, though the pressure on McClaren of knowing how strongly Nixon felt remained. Further, the White House tapes of the conversation seem to indicate that Nixon was more solicitous of the wishes of big business in general than aware of the beneficent intentions of ITT towards his party's convention. In the telephone conversation of 21 April with Kleindienst, Nixon said;

Well, I have, I have nothing to do with them (ITT) and I want something clearly understood and if it is not understood, McClaren's ass is to be out within one hour. The ITT thing—stay the hell out of it.

I do not want McClaren to run around prosecuting people raising hell about conglomerates stirring things up at this point.[36]

In the meeting with Mitchell at which the formal order was rescinded, Nixon said: 'I don't care about the ITT,' but added: 'The business community believes we are a hell of a lot rougher on them in the anti-trust than our predecessors were.'

Assuming that Nixon was being honest in the conversations on the White House tapes—and the unguarded style of his remarks argues in that direction—it would seem that ITT's general arguments rather than the Convention bribe were crucial. On the other hand, the extraordinary degree of access to decision makers ITT enjoyed—which allowed it to make the argument successfully—was almost certainly aided by the proffered bribe.

ITT's contacts with the Administration in protection of its interests in Chile show much the same pattern of ready access to stopping government officials and a readiness on the part of the Administration to meet the wishes of ITT.[37] Once more a campaign of top-level lobbying was mounted, paying particular attention to Ehrlichman and the office of the National Security Adviser, Henry Kissinger. ITT wished to persuade the government to take a strong line as it believed that the State Department was going too 'soft' on Allende. As ITT itself had failed to arrange a blockade of Chile by securing agreements not to supply Allende, ITT wished the government to take over the task. Further, ITT wished to develop an alliance with the Central Intelligence Agency against Allende which went back to an earlier attempt by Allende to win the Presidency of Chile in 1964. (In 1964 the CIA had provided funds for Allende's chief opponent equivalent to 60 per cent of his opponent's total budget.) Meetings were held between ITT officials and the CIA in the form of both its director, Richard Helms, and the CIA's chief of clandestine activities in Latin America, William Broe. John McCone, a director of ITT, was a former Director of the CIA. The ITT offered funds to the CIA to conduct activities against Allende, an offer the CIA apparently turned down because it wished to use properly appropriated funds. The CIA did, however, advise ITT on how to deploy its funds to the best effect against Allende. The CIA could not be hired by ITT, but was certainly willing to help ITT with advice on how to block Allende.

American action against Allende was severe. The United States did all in its power to exacerbate the economic crisis which Allende's economic policies produced. The policy of the United States towards the Allende government was influenced by both economic and strategic factors and not just by the lobbying of ITT and other major corporations. None the less, the severity of the administration's policy—which included approval of assassination attempts and providing weapons for a group who planned to murder the Chilean Chief of Staff, General

Schneider, who was a major obstacle to a military coup—was welcome to ITT. The general direction of American policy, the centrality of securing compensation of ITT in the list of American objectives in Chile, and the campaign of economic warfare against Chile were all welcome to ITT. The concurrence of the policy of the Administration and ITT towards Allende was surely aided by the frequent and close consultations between ITT and the government which were perhaps more consistent with élite theory than with pluralist politics.[38]

The Breakdown of the System

By the mid 1970s, American businessmen had become sharply aware of the need to recast the form of business involvement in politics. A combination of factors had made change necessary, while good fortune produced a change in the law which made adaptation easy.

The Watergate affair marked the end of the old form of business involvement in politics. The most obvious reason for this was the activity of the Watergate Senate Committee, the Watergate Special Prosecutors, and the Security and Exchange Commission. The enquiries of the Ervin Senate Committee into the affairs of the Finance Committee to Re-Elect the President (FCRP) unmasked some of the illegal payments made to the Nixon campaign by corporations such as Ashland Oil and the American Shipbuilding Corporation. The Special Prosecutors whom Nixon had been forced to appoint to bring to trial criminals involved in the Watergate affair succeeded in flushing out many of the corporations which had made illegal payments to the FCRP partly by investigations and partly by making it clear that while confessions of guilt would not secure immunity from prosecution, they would mitigate the zeal with which malefactors were pursued. Spurred on by the example of the Special Prosecutors, the Securities and Exchange Commission (SEC), which superintends financial dealings in the United States, basing its enquiries on the somewhat slender pretext that the illegal payments involved deceit of shareholders (as the payments naturally did not appear in company accounts), proceeded to unveil the massive extent of illegal payments to political campaigns within the USA and of bribery of politicians and officials abroad. It is likely that these revelations would have severely curtailed such practices at any time; after Watergate, the stress on 'clean politics' within the USA made change imperative.

Businessmen were also eager to end illegal payments because the system had been developed by the FCRP into a major form of blackmail. It will be recalled that firms such as Minnesota Mining and Manufacturing had typically made numerous small-scale payments to politicians. As in so many other ways, the Nixon campaign people had taken established abuses of the electoral system and magnified them many times. In place of making judicious small payments to a range of politicians, corporations found that they were being assessed by the FCRP for significant sums of money with the clear message that failure to pay would result in the imposition of sanctions. The FCRP had turned the campaign-contribution system into an illegal form of taxation. Once again the example of Gulf Oil serves to make a general point, as the following extract from the Senate Watergate Committee hearings suggests.

Senator Ervin: How did you figure that the best interests of Gulf would be protected by making a contribution? Mr. Wild: I arrived at the decision that if we were going to be treated in an equal way, I knew other corporations were going to—a big effort was going to be made and if there were not some participation on my part or our part we may be, you know, whether on some blacklist or bottom of the totem pole. I would just like [someone] to answer my telephone calls once in a while and that may not happen sometimes.[39]

Wild pointed out that the Administration had numerous opportunities to harass his company: 'There are 61 agencies of Government that have something to do with our business, unfortunately.' It was much the same with another transgressor, American Airlines, which was approached for a contribution by Herb Kalmbach, a White House staff member who, as if to make the dangers of refusing to contribute clear, had worked for United Airlines, American's rival. The former Chief Executive Officer of American, George Spater, argued that 'most contributions from the business community are not volunteered to seek competitive advantage but are made in response to pressure for fear of competitive disadvantage.'[40] Amongst the issues American had before the government at the time was a plan to acquire Western Airlines, a move which the government had the power to block. The menace behind the requests for contributions to the FCRP was made clear by the rank of government officials requesting the money; Ashland Oil had the experience of being solicited for contributions for the first time by a Cabinet Secretary, Maurice Stans, Commerce Secretary.[41] In brief, far from Watergate marking business being in control of politicians, it showed how the cosy purchase of access by corporations was on the verge of being an escalating form of blackmail.

Just as the old system of business involvement in politics was dying, the need for businessmen to be involved in politics became greater, or was felt to be greater. Partly because of Watergate, and partly for other longer-term reasons, the Republican Party was in a poor position both in terms of the proportion of the electorate which identified with it, and in terms of the number of Congressional seats it held. As Republican legislators are by far the most likely to side with management, this was a serious matter for businessmen. Schattschneider had already pointed out that the political success of American business was linked closely to the support of business by the Republican Party. Now the Republican Party was in such a weak state that many feared for its future. Conversely, the 1974 elections brought to office a large number of liberal Democrats who businessmen feared—probably erroneously—would take a hostile view of their interests.

Even more important was the rise of the public interest groups which we discuss in the next chapter. Whether there is any fundamental conflict of interest between public interest groups and business is perhaps a moot point; so long as all manufacturers are obliged to spend an equal amount on producing safe cars, additional costs may be passed onto the consumer. However, businessmen felt that both consumer and environmental groups provided a major challenge at least to the way in which business was conducted, if not to capitalism itself. Environmental groups have been able to obtain legislation such as the Endangered Species Act which they have been able to use to block many projects corporations favour. Even the development of the Alaskan oil fields was delayed by opposition from environmental groups until the AOPEC embargo and the OPEC price increases tilted the balance back to the oil companies. Oil companies suffered another setback when the oil-depletion allowance, almost the perfect symbol of unwonted government beneficence to business, was abolished by Congress in 1975. Moreover, public interest groups such as Common Cause had played a major part in unmasking the illegal payments made by corporations to politicians, and this was scarcely likely to endear them to businessmen.

The passing of legislation to protect endangered species and institute stricter controls of industrial pollution and safety (including safety at work) exemplified the weakness in the old system of business political representation. That system was one in which, as Epstein had noted,[42] corporations, by a variety of tactics, pursued their own interests. It was not a system which provided well for the representation of the collective interests of corporations. What was the concern of every corporation was likely to be the concern of none. Peak associations were weak, and lobbyists for individual corporations likely to think about issues which particularly affected their own corporations. Much of the legislation which was unwelcome to the business community but supported by public interest groups was in a way not so much imposed on business after a fight, but slipped through without business noticing. The old relationship between business and politics had existed at a time when business was relatively immune from public criticism, and did not need to concern itself with any but the most detailed of issues. As criticism of business increased with the growth of public interest groups, and as public confidence in business leaders fell (along with confidence in most other prominent institutions in the USA), business found itself in a new political situation. Businessmen felt under attack from public interest groups, unpopular with the electorate as a whole, and short of friends in the Congress. A new political strategy was needed.

Recent Developments

Almost at the very moment that it became too risky for corporations to buy access illegally, the law was changed. Corporations had done little to bring about this change in the law. Indeed, corporations were the almost unnoticed beneficiaries of legislation intended primarily to help unions out of a tight legal spot. In 1968 the Justice Department indicted officers of a local of the pipefitters' union for a violation of the election laws by coercing supposedly voluntary contributions by the use of a predetermined formula. As the case was one of legal novelty and complexity, it progressed towards the Supreme Court, where unions feared a ruling might be given which would compromise the position of union political action committees (PACS). Representative Orville Hanson introduced legislation to safeguard the position of union PACs, and, though there was no pressure from corporations (many of which were still running secret, illegal funds) it included corporation PACs in order to ward off serious opposition to the bill, there being little time to spare. Few expected corporations to take advantage of the law because they had shown so little interest in PACs in the past. The act made a crucial change in the law, however. Corporations were allowed to pay the costs of establishing and administering PACs which solicited contributions from executives and shareholders. This crucial change was confirmed by Congress in the 1974 Federal Campaign Finance Act Amendment. Two rulings by the Federal Elections Commission (FEC) gave corporations a temporary additional incentive to form PACs. First, in an advisory opinion requested by Sun Oil, the FEC ruled that PACs run by corporations could solicit contributions from employees as well as from shareholders. Second, the FEC allowed corporations to establish more than one PAC. As PACs are limited in the amount they can contribute to any one campaign— to $5,000--this seemed to open the way to unlimited contributions to campaigns from businessmen simply by the founding of additional PACs. Both these rulings by the FEC were modified by Congress in 1976. Corporations and unions were limited to two 'crossovers' per year in which corporations could solicit funds from workers and unions could solicit from shareholders. Corporations, in the so-called non-proliferation clause, were limited to one PAC per firm. None the less, the law was more favourable to business PACs than before, and the FEC rulings had given a particularly sharp initial incentive to corporations to form PACs.

The growth of business PACs has been rapid. In the first ten weeks of 1976 100 business PACs registered with the FEC, and by March 1976 business PACs had $9 million to hand. In spite of modification of the FEC's rulings by Congress, the growth of corporate contributions to campaigns has been immense. Between 1974 and 1976 legal contributions from corporations to political campaigns rose from $2.5 million to $7.1 million.[43] Within a few years corporations had become almost as significant a source of campaign funds as unions, and showed every sign of out-stripping them in the future. One corporation, General Electric, raised a political warchest of $75,000 within six months by an appeal to 531 of its executives. This was a sum standing comparison with election-year expenditures of the illegal business campaign funds. In general, 'going legal' coincided with a considerable increase, not a decrease, in business expenditure on politics. In 1978, there were 776 PACs linked to corporations compared with 89 in 1974. Their contributions to campaigns totalled $8 million, about the same as those of the unions, and equivalent to 15 per cent of total campaign receipts.

The form of strategy that business PACs have followed has not been what was anticipated. Most politicians, with either apprehension or anticipation, depending on whether they were liberal or conservative, expected business PACs to benefit the more conservative, overtly pro-management politicians. The adoption of federal financing for Presidential elections meant that business PACs, like all others, have been obliged to devote their funds to Congressional elections. Congress shows few signs of being prepared to adopt federal financing for Congressional elections. Congressional conservatives have not benefited much from the creation of business PACs, however. Business money has gone to a wide variety of politicians. Thus the beneficiaries of General Electric's PAC in 1976 included Edward Kennedy and Hubert Humphrey as well as President Ford and James Buckley.[44] Overall, the business PACs gave almost as much money— probably 40 per cent of their funds— to liberal Democrats as they gave to conservatives. The conservative *Right Report* found that in 117 key congressional districts in 1976, business was on the same side as organized labour and that both were supporting liberals. Conservatives feel hard done by, and suspect that their supposed allies in business have forgotten their political principles.[45] The *Washington Monthly* quoted Representative Robert Dorman, a conservative Republican: 'Corporate managers are whores. They don't care who's in office, what party or what they stand for. They're just out to buy you.'[46] Senator Laxalt (R., Nevada) saw a deep motive for this alliance, for once agreeing with the radicals. 'It's one big political bed. If tomorrow it was announced that all government intervention in business were ended, there would be coronaries in every boardroom.'[47] In short, big business does not identify its interests with conservatism. The *Congressional Quarterly* commented;

When the new conservative thinks about a low tax economic climate in which business can flourish, they are talking primarily about small business. The link between large corporations and conservative Republicans is just about gone. Disaffection between the corporations and the right, smoldering for years, turned into open hostility after campaign finance reports for the 1976 elections showed conservatives just where business was putting its money.[48]

The truth of the matter is that business political contributions flow not only to conservatives, but to those with power. In recent years the seniority system, long the bane of liberals, started to work to their advantage and produce more and more liberal committee chairmen. Moreover, those making political contributions for reasons of self-interest like to make a safe bet. Corporations like to give money to incumbents because incumbents are the most likely to be re-elected, and the incumbents are usually (in the House by a margin of 2 : 1) Democrats. In fact, business PACs give three-quarters of their money to incumbents. Primary beneficiaries of corporations' political spending have been committee chairmen. In 1976 PACs gave contributions equivalent to 60 per cent of their expenses to the campaigns of House Committee chairmen and equivalent to 20 per cent of the campaign costs of Senate committee chairmen.[49] The problem which faces managers of business PACs was summarized by the Vice-President of one Wisconsin firm responsible for Governmental Affairs. On the one hand, the local Representative, Henry Reuss, was thought to be too liberal. On the other hand, Reuss was not only certain to be re-elected but was Chairman of a House Committee, Banking and Currency, which had a major impact on the firm's industry. The corporation's PAC gave Reuss the maximum possible contribution, $5,000, and hoped that gradually his ideas would mellow. At least the firm could be sure of an attentive hearing from Reuss.

This offers an interesting contrast with the behaviour of the older business pressure groups. Whereas the Chamber of Commerce and the National Association of Manufacturers were always thought to be highly ideological organizations, the new

business PACs have been highly pragmatic in their behaviour.
All the signs are that the business PACs will be all the more
successful for this. The new business PACs are more like such
European pressure groups as the Confederation of British
Industries, recognizing the need to adapt their arguments to the
politician in power. Like the CBI, the business PACs are finding
that such a strategy does not mean being without influence.

Business Lobbying

Just as the new political action committees proved a novel and
extensive opportunity for businessmen to influence electoral
politics, so the lobbying effort made by business has been
refined and increased.

We should recall that the most prominent of the business
lobbies in the 1950s and 1960s, the Chamber of Commerce and
the National Association of Manufacturers, were poorly
regarded in Washington. As late as 1969, the Chamber was still
regarded as an ideological warrior. By 1976 it had moved sufficiently to come out in favour of projects normally associated
with liberals, such as day-care centres and temporary public-
service jobs to counteract unemployment.

This change of image coincides with more fundamental
changes in the Chamber, which has been growing rapidly.
Whereas the Chamber had 35,686 members in 1967, by 1976 it
had over 61,578 of which 57,994 were individual concerns. As
400 of the *Fortune* 500—the 500 most important corporations
listed by *Fortune* magazine—belong, the Chamber has a claim
to represent big business as well as its traditional 'Main Street'
constituency.[50] However, smaller enterprises continue to dominate the running of the Chamber; only sixteen of the sixty-three
directors represent larger concerns. The Chamber's status as
the major business forum would have been further enhanced if
merger with the NAM had been achieved; however, the two
have merged in seventeen states.

The Chamber of Commerce has been revivified not only in
terms of image and membership but in terms of the skill of its
lobbyists. Current reports suggest that business lobbyists have
become a significant influence on Congress. One commentator
argued: 'On a day to day basis they do not balance labour', but

he noted that in specific campaigns, the Chamber can be a very powerful force.[51] The Chamber has been one of the earliest practitioners of grass-roots lobbying, a technique gaining many adherents in Washington. Instead of leaving the presentation of an interests case to professionals—the practice favoured in the past—interest groups either bring people to Washington to see their legislators or—and preferably—encourage their members to contact legislators during their increasingly frequent visits back to their constituency. Grass-roots lobbying was a technique disparaged in the 1950s when Bauer, Pool, and Dexter carried out their study; in the more populist 1970s it is almost obligatory for lobbies.

It may seem perverse that a business organization should become a leading exponent of grass-roots lobbying. There are two reasons why the Chamber of Commerce finds the technique congenial. First, though the Chamber is financially dependent on subscriptions from the large corporations such as Du Pont, which pay $50,000 a year each, it also contains many small businessmen who, by virtue of their social position in many communities, are well placed to try to persuade decision-makers. Second, the Chamber with branches in every Congressional district can draw the attention to what in the introductory chapter was referred to as a structural constraint—the impact of employment and prosperity in that area if 'anti-business' legislation is adopted. 'In the last four or five years, business has made significant strides in being more effective—primarily by getting over the arguments to members couched in terms of the impact on a member's constitutents.' Many members who may vote, for say, an environmental protection measure, do not do so when it is pointed out what effect this will have on a large employer in their district.

The Chamber of Commerce has advanced far in the 1970s. Yet certain weaknesses remain, and it has not yet attained the status of the CBI in Britain or of employers' organizations in countries such as Sweden and West Germany. Nor is it likely to. There are several reasons for this. First, the Chamber has not cast off entirely its ideological style, as perhaps may be judged by the comment from one of its leaders: 'The mainstream of the business community is more concerned about the survival of capitalism than at any time in history. I'm talking about the middle of the road businessman. They feel we are following step by step the path of the United Kingdom and other countries.' Second, links with the Executive branch are still weak, even if those with Congress are stronger. The *National Journal* commented: 'Little time is spent trying to influence policy making within the Executive Branch. This was true when the Democrats were in power as it is now with the Republicans in control.'[53] One of the Chamber's officials inadvertently illustrated the point the *National Journal* was making when he described links between the Chamber and the Executive by saying that Chamber of Commerce officials had lunch once a month with the Secretary of Commerce.[54] As the Secretary of Commerce is the Cabinet Secretary supposedly in closest touch with the business community, this was scarcely the ready access to government that European employers' organizations expect. Third, large corporations are not prepared to entrust their political representation to the Chamber, feeling that it is still too committed to small business. Many corporations belong to the Chamber merely *pro forma*, or as one executive put it, 'You belong to the Chamber like you go to church'[55]—out of a limited sense of duty. Large corporations continue to expand their individual representation in Washington at a prodigious rate. The number of lobbyists for corporations in Washington has grown from 8,000 to 15,000 in the last five years. But it is not merely that large corporations feel that they need to protect only their individual interests outside the Chamber of Commerce. Large corporations have banded together to form perhaps the most interesting of the business pressure groups, the Business Roundtable.

The Business Roundtable

The founding of the Business Roundtable in 1972 was perhaps the most significant sign of the political vulnerability which American businessmen felt in the early 1970s: 180 corporations, all in the *Fortune* 500, belong. The purpose of the organization is to pool the resources of large corporations in the pursuit of political matters of joint concern. It is an important aspect of the style of the Business Roundtable that participation in its meetings is limited to the Chief Executive Officer of each member corporation, and that these officials are fully involved in the political work of the organization. The *National Journal* said of one of the most important members of the Roundtable, Irving Shapiro of Du Pont, that he 'is the very model of the modern business leader—with one foot in the boardroom and the other in Washington.'[56]

The Business Roundtable's budget is small—only $2 million per annum— and companies contribute $2,500 to $40,000 per annum. However, partly because the Roundtable draws on the resources of member corporations, this has not prevented it from becoming a very highly regarded lobby.[57] Eschewing highly ideological politics in the style of the old Chamber or NAM, the Roundtable has a reputation for making 'common-sense' arguments which can appeal to a variety of legislators. It also has a reputation for expertise, reflecting its successful deployment of the resources of member organizations. A leader of the Democratic Party in Congress commented after a meeting with officers of the Roundtable: 'They knew their stuff. They had their figures.' The older business lobbies had not always. Representative Richard Preyer, (D., North Carolina) commented: 'I have been impressed with the quality of their research.'[58] The Roundtable, similar in this use of expertise to the European employers' organizations, is similar too in following a strategy of 'articulate advocacy of a limited agenda.' Undoubtedly, too, as Lindblom would predict, the Roundtable spokesmen have a prestige unmatched by ordinary pressure group lobbyists. A Democratic Congressman, Benjamin Spirer (New York) commented, 'You can be sure that there would be very few members of Congress who would not meet with the President of a Business Roundtable corporation even if there was no district connection.'[59] Corporation chiefs are men of consequence, not just lobbyists.

The Business Roundtable also has much better links to the Executive than the Chamber has. Though President Carter declined to meet the Business Roundtable policy committee before the election, he has had several meetings with its officials, particularly with Shapiro. Contacts are maintained not only with the Secretary of the Treasury (Blumenthal) and Commerce (Krepps), natural links between business and government, but also with such White House staff members as E. Stuart Eizenstat (Domestic Policy Adviser).[60] In an age of a powerful Executive, this seems wise.

The Pay Off

American businessmen may well have expected to do poorly politically in the mid 1970s. Liberal Democrats made massive gains in the 1974 midterm elections which were not reversed in either 1976 or 1978. Attacks on such features of the Congressional scene as the seniority system further weakened the position of conservatives. The election of a Democrat, President Carter, in 1976 seemed to reproduce the features of American politics which in 1964–6 allowed the adoption of a mass of liberal legislation. Yet, contrary to these expectations, business has done extremely well politically in recent times. Labour unions have failed to achieve any of their major objectives. Reform of the laws regulating union recognition and organization, and also of picketing on construction sites, have been rejected. In February 1978, the consumer movement, apparently so strong in the early 1970s, suffered a major reverse when a proposal to establish an agency to represent the interests of consumers was rejected. The triumph of business on these issues was due to a number of factors, including, on the labour issues, some mis-calculations by unions. Moreover, the new, supposedly liberal, Democrats have turned out to be conservative on many issues and, to the delight of businessmen, the mood of the country has been interpreted by commentators as increasingly conservative. But the most proximate cause of business's triumphs over consumers and labour unions was the improved political per-formance of business. After the unexpected defeat of the proposal to establish a consumer-advocacy agency Speaker O'Neill des-cribed the business campaign against it as the most intense he had seen in twenty-five years.[61] Grass-roots lobbying techniques were used extensively in attempts to defeat the agency, while the Business Roundtable added its own more distant but auth-oritative voice.

The story of business involvement in politics in the 1970s is a fascinating illustration of how American business has learnt rapidly and cleverly how to protect its interests in the changed political circumstances of that decade. Business has succeeded in restoring its pre-eminent position politically, and recent 'tax revolts' have further strengthened its position. The vulnerability of business to attacks from labour and public interest groups, which seemed a growing problem to corporations in the early 1970s, has been ended. The period from about 1968 to 1975 when businessmen found themselves increasingly surrounded by uncongenial legislation seems to corporation executives already almost a nightmare, a temporary interruption of the privileged position of business in American society.

Yet the apparent continuity in the political position of business in the United States since 1952 should not distract our attention from the very different form that the relationship between business and politics has taken. Put simply, business has been forced to play pluralist politics. Hundreds of corporations and associations of smaller businesses have formed Political Action Committees to defend their interests. At least one 'peak' association, the Chamber of Commerce, has been rejuvenated. Even large corporations have been forced to recognize that the collective interests of business need defending and accordingly have joined together, partly in the Chamber and partly in the Business Roundtable, so that they may have a greater effect on government. Meanwhile, individual corporations continue to expand their representation in Washington, and we have seen that in the last five years (1974–9) there has been almost a 100 per cent increase in the number of corporation lobbyists in Washington.[62]

To individual corporations these changes may matter little so long as business wins its political battles, which it certainly is doing at present. The corporation staff may have to be expanded in order to take on lobbyists and a Vice-President for Governmental Affairs; expenditure may increase as subscriptions are taken out to the Business Roundtable or the Chamber of Commerce. In terms of a corporation's total budget, these expenses are trivial. Indeed, powerful corporations, such as Mobil, are able to undertake an extensive advertising campaign aimed at raising the popularity of business with the public in general. Yet the significance of the changes for us is certain. In the 1950s American business could afford to ignore politics. In a manner which Lukes would explain in terms of false consciousness, the climate of opinion was so favourable to business that no great political effort was required. In the 1960s business became more involved in politics, partly by conventional lobbying but to a considerable extent by veiled illegal contributions to political campaigns and secret maneouvring with political élites. By the early 1970s business had come to feel that common business interests were under attack and that it was necessary to turn to the classic techniques of pluralist politics—lobbying and Political Action Committees—to defend itself. Of course, business has many advantages which ordinary pressure groups have not, including massive financial resources and research facilities. Moreover, as Lindblom has argued, the costs to the community of defying the political wishes of business are far in excess of defying an ordinary pressure group. Yet there had been a change. In the 1950s businessmen did not need to sully their hands with conventional politics. Now they do; even though American business has learnt how to play pluralist politics brilliantly, its new-found need to be politically involved is significant.

The Voluntary Interest Groups

The groups we have examined so far have been based on occupational categories. Sometimes membership in occupational groups is more or less compulsory; unions, for example, frequently maintain 'closed shops' in which all who wish to work in the industry must join the union. In other cases—notably the farmers' organizations—membership is advantageous for occupational reasons, such as the use of a grain elevator. The groups we shall look at here are groups which, though they often offer incentives for individuals to join, are groups people choose to join because to some extent they support the group's objectives, or at least identify with its general concerns. It is the prominence of these non-occupational groups that has prompted people to think of the USA as a country in which interest groups are particularly important. There are, however many different types of non-occupational groups. In particular, groups vary in the range of issues which concern them. A distinction will be drawn between public interest groups, organizations working in a policy area of benefit to the whole community (such as honesty in government), and single issue groups which, as their name implies, have a narrower focus.

The Public Interest Groups

One of the best-known objections to pluralism is that though there are interest groups to defend sectional interests such as those of farmers, workers, and employers, there are no interest groups to defend the concerns of all. This apparently plausible claim has never been entirely true of the USA, and has become less so. Throughout American history a number of organizations seeking to further their conception of the public good rather than the material advantage of their members have flourished. The Anti-Slavery movement was perhaps the most important in the nineteenth century; in the twentieth century the Anti-Saloon League and other teetotal groups secured a constitutional amendment (the 18th) prohibiting the sale of alcoholic drink. The Progressive movement, which worked for measures to increase the honesty and efficiency of government, has left its mark on local, state, and even federal government in the form of a series of institutional reforms and changes. Two of the best-known public interest groups operating today, the Audubon Society (an environmental group) and the League of Women Voters (a group working for governmental reform and a limited number of liberal causes) had their origins in 1905 and 1920 respectively, and are thus as old as many of the economic interest groups.

Yet most commentators would agree that the late 1960s witnessed a dramatic increase in the number, size, and effectiveness of public interest groups. Common Cause, the best known of the new public interest groups had its origins in the attempts in the late 1960s of a group which included former Secretary of Health Education and Welfare John Gardner to find an effective way to promote honesty and efficiency in government. In 1970 the group launched Common Cause as a mass membership organization; by 1974, Common Cause had 325,000 members.[1] Ralph Nader shot to prominence in 1966 after his book *Unsafe at Any Speed*[2] had highlighted dangerous design defects in a popular General Motors model. General Motors contributed to making Nader a prominent public figure by the clumsiness of their reply; instead of replying to Nader's technical comments, General Motors hired private detectives to follow Nader in an unsuccessful attempt to uncover compromising details about his private life. By the early 1970s, Nader ran a variety of groups linked loosely through his Public Citizen Foundation, covering a wide range of industries and consumer products; one group, Congress Watch, even extended consumerism into the political domain. Nader's Public Citizen Foundation soon attained 175,000 contributors. New environmental-protection groups such as Friends of the Earth and the Sierra Club also boomed. In the mid 1970s, the Sierra Club had 153,000 members. Older public interest groups were rejuvenated. Membership in the Audubon Society increased sharply—apparently to its own surprise—while the League of Women Voters claimed 160,000 members, and the Consumers' Union 285,000.[3]

With such large memberships, public interest groups could deploy significant resources to advance their causes. In 1974 Common Cause had a budget of $6.6 million and in the same year Public Citizen raised $1.2 million.[4] As public interest groups also benefit from an unusually high willingness of their membership to work voluntarily for the organization—at least 10 per cent of the membership of Common Cause is active on its behalf[5]—such budgets allow public interest groups to support significant political activity.

Why the public interest groups blossomed in the late 1960s is an interesting question. Indeed, to some political scientists the existence of public interest groups at all is a puzzle. Mancur Olson has argued that people join interest groups only when there is some individualized benefit available only to members.[6] There is no reason why a farmer, for example, should join an agricultural pressure group; he will receive farm subsidies whether or not he belongs. Moreover, as but one potential member amongst many, he cannot assume that his decision to belong will affect others. Olson argues that interest groups must either secure compulsory membership (by methods such as the closed shop for trade unions) or provide benefits such as the use of grain elevators or cheap insurance available only to members of the group. Olson's arguments seem to have special importance for public interest groups. If it is possible to persuade people to join interest groups which promote their economic well-being only by offering selective benefits limited to members, how is it possible to persuade people to join interest groups which are not designed to promote their economic well-being? One answer is that people join interest groups —even economic interest groups— partly out of a sense of loyalty or idealism, which Olson can recognize only by stretching his theory to cover psychological benefits of belonging. As we have noted, public interest groups have been able to draw on such idealism throughout American history. Moreover, as Berry shows,[7] a significant proportion of public interest groups—perhaps 30 per cent—do not have members at all but are financed by foundations or bequests; the wealth of the United States is put to diverse purposes. But as Olson would predict, many public interest groups do in fact provide some service to members only. Some organizations provide only an attractive magazine—as does the Sierra Club; others, such as the consumer groups, provide members with reports on product safety and reliability which can save the members' family far more than the cost of membership. But though Berry found that 10 per cent of public interest groups provided services and 76 per cent a publication, his overall conclusion was that neither the services nor the publications seemed an adequate explanation for membership.[8] It seems once more that idealism cannot be neglected completely in explaining political action.

Why public interest groups blossomed in the late 1960s is a different matter, and one which is most convincingly addressed by MacFarland.[9] Several well-known changes in American politics help to answer the question. First, the electorate in general showed a greater awareness of political issues and a weakened loyalty to political parties. In elections, this ensured that more voters responded to campaign issues and fewer to party identification. The result of change was in turn that there was more scope for public interest groups, which by definition stress issues outside the framework of political parties. Second, the affluence of America since World War II has made it easier for organizations like the Sierra Club to raise questions about the quality of life as opposed to questions about primary concerns such as employment, wages, and housing. (Of course this is not to suggest that such questions are irrelevant to all Americans.) Third, though the willingness of Americans in general to participate in politics has been declining, there is evidence that middle-class Americans—who of course are less interested in measures to meet primary needs such as employment—have become more willing to participate in politics. Fifth, technological change has aided public interest groups. WATS telephone lines enable an unlimited number of calls to be made at no extra cost; computerized mailing lists aid the soliciting of funds and recruiting of members from national offices without local organizations first having to be established.

Some have attached particular importance to the role of political entrepreneurs in taking advantage of these changes.

Thus Salisbury argues that whether or not a group succeeds depends on the quality of the entrepreneur who establishes it.[10] An able entrepreneur such as Nader or Gardner will establish a strong group. Yet Salisbury's theory clearly does not take us very far. Of course the charismatic qualities of Nader and Gardner were an immense advantage to the Public Citizen and Common Cause groups. Yet in different times Gardner would have remained in party politics, and Nader might have run for Congress; if they had tried to form public interest groups, no one would have been interested. The fundamental reason why public interest groups became viable was surely the wave of scepticism about all its major institutions which swept the United States in the 1960s and 1970s. Even before the Watergate affair, the Michigan surveys had recorded a substantial decline in what is called 'trust in government'—a set of answers to questions in which respondents reply that their leaders genuinely seek the public good and are not dominated by either the wish to enrich themselves or work for 'special interests'. Between 1958 and 1972 the proportion of sceptics rose from 22 to 45 per cent.[11] Watergate did little to improve matters. Indeed, Watergate was a godsend to Common Cause, seemingly demonstrating that Common Cause's arguments for reform of the political system were timely. An even more precipitate decline occurred in public confidence in business. In 1968 Yankelovich had found that 70 per cent of Americans agreed with the claim that 'Business tries to strike a fair balance between profits and the interest of the public.' The proportion agreeing with this claim fell to 33 per cent in 1970 and 18 per cent in 1975. Similarly, Louis Harris had found that 55 per cent of the public had confidence in the leaders of major companies; by 1971 the proportion had fallen to 27 per cent.[12] Again, Watergate did little to change the picture, and Congressional hearings produced numerous examples of corrupt and illegal pressures from business on government. Some dramatic accidents—like the oil spill off Santa Barbara in 1969—seemed to show that not just government was in danger of despoliation by business.

Yet though the public had lost confidence in politicians and business leaders, there was little support for radical change. Indeed, 90 per cent of the sample interviewed by Yankelovich in the poll mentioned above were prepared to make sacrifices to save 'the free enterprise system'. Another poll carried out by Yankelovich in 1977 showed that by 62 to 14 per cent the respondents rejected the claim, 'We would all be better off if the government had more control over the economy', and by 52 to 16 per cent the same respondents rejected the claim that the 'free enterprise system benefits the few.'[13] In short, while the public distrusted the behaviour of both industry and government leaders, it remained overwhelmingly loyal to the system as such. This was an ideal environment in which public interest groups could operate, offering potential solutions to abuses through limited reform, rather than through fundamental change. These changes in public opinion could be reinforced by public interest groups. However, the scepticism of the American public about the working of their institutions occurred before interest groups who benefited from it were particularly strong. Moreover, such shifts in public opinion are not to be explained by interest-group activity alone, or indeed, to any significant extent.

The Concerns of Public Interest Groups

The very large number of public interest groups makes it inevitably difficult to generalize about their concerns. Businessmen, on the principle that they should know their enemy, are issued with a booklet which lists literally hundreds of different public interest groups and describes their attitudes. Some are described as reasonable or moderate; others are seen as implacable enemies of free enterprise. The major public interest groups specialize quite distinctly in their concerns. Common Cause has focused almost exclusively on reforming the machinery of government, including the election laws. Its best-known and proudest success has been the adoption of campaign-finance reform, including requirements for the disclosure of contributions and federal financing of Presidential elections. To its great embarrassment, the Nixon Committee to Re-Elect the President (CREEP) was forced by a Common Cause lawsuit to disclose all its contributors, a major step in the unravelling of Watergate. At present, Common Cause is pressing hard for the extension of federal financing to Congressional elections, a measure thought by some Congressmen to have a 50 per cent chance of success in

the next few years. Other Common Cause concerns have included measures to increase the efficiency and representatives
of Congress through changes in the committee system and
departures from seniority.

On only a few occasions did Common Cause stray into a
substantive policy area. In 1970 and 1971 Common Cause
worked to force the Congressional leadership to allow a vote to
repeal the Gulf of Tonkin resolution, used by Presidents Johnson
and Nixon as legal authority for American participation in the
Vietnam War, though probably not intended as such by
Congress. More recently, Common Cause has advocated changes
in the federal income-tax system which is so inequitable that
many large corporations pay no tax at all. Common Cause is
considering a new range of issues aimed at what it considers
wasteful government programmes obtained by special interests.
Yet such campaigns may well make Common Cause even less
popular with liberal groups who see their favourite programmes,
such as job-creation schemes threatened. Yet by and large,
Common Cause's objectives are to do with the processes rather
than the substance of politics, with the machinery rather than
the outputs of the policy process.

In contrast, Nader and his Public Citizen groups are very
much concerned with the substance of policy. Nader's reputation rests on the work he has done to protect consumers,
beginning with the report on the Corvair, *Unsafe at Any Speed*.
Nader organizations have expanded into some issues of environmental policy, notably the controversy over the safety (or
danger) of atomic power stations. However, Nader's Congress
Watch project which attempted to monitor the performance of
every Congressional committee—and ultimately of every
legislator—was conspicuously unsuccessful. Nader himself was
to describe the project as 'my C 5A'[14]—a reference to a notori-
ously expensive aircraft project. Errors made by the researchers
working on the project were of course quickly noted by Congress,
and contributed to a noticeable reduction in Nader's standing.
Yet Nader remains the personality in public interest politics
with the most coherent and interesting political thought. His
analysis of American society is radical. Nader sees all aspects of
American society—government, environment, universities,
and even the thought of individual citizens—being influenced

and corrupted by business corporations. But Nader's solutions are more in the American tradition than in that of the European left. The individual citizen retains the responsibility and the capacity to shake off many of the baneful consequences of business. In personal decisions, the individual can turn away from products such as junk food and even alcohol injurious to health; by collective action, the citizenry can call successfully to task irresponsible corporations without transforming society. Ultimate solutions include measures to make control of large companies by shareholders more of a reality, the appointment of representatives of the public interest to the boards of companies, and the fostering of smaller enterprises, including co-operatives. Here is no recipe for socialism.

The environmental groups are perhaps the most differentiated of the public interest groups. Conservation has been an issue in the United States throughout this century; Theodore Roosevelt claimed to be a conservationist. The ruthless despoliation of the environment which contrasts with the beauty of the West and the Appalachians would seem to make the existence of the issue obvious. Yet the meaning of the issue has changed. For Roosevelt, conservation meant preserving natural resources so that they could be exploited more efficiently or profitably at a later date, a policy particularly associated with federal forests.[15] The environmentalists who emerged in the 1960s in constrast had as their immediate objectives the control of pollution from factories, power stations, cars, and houses. Controlling pollution has costs as well as benefits. A further distinguishing feature of the modern environmentalists is that they are willing to accept a high ratio of costs to benefits, and even to sacrifice economic growth in order to attain their goals. The belief that there are 'limits to growth' and that the United States has attained an aggregate level of prosperity sufficient to allow it to sacrifice economic growth to the cause of a cleaner environment was more clearly held in some quarters than others. For example, the Friends of the Earth were more 'extreme' in this respect than the Sierra Club. Yet even the Sierra Club found it difficult to accept any of the plausible alternatives to the solution of the energy problem; both atomic power and the expansion of coal mining were objectionable.[16]

What is the 'public interest' which Public Interest Groups pursue?

Many commentators trace the intellectual origins of the public interest groups back to the Progressive movement, and reforms such as the 'city manager' idea which sought to replace the often corrupt manoeuvrings of politicians with the rule of dispassionate experts. The public interest was to be pursued by taking politics out of government. Progressives have been criticized and derided for this view ever since. It has often been argued by historians that the city managers' view of the public interest was suspiciously in line with the middle class's interests, emphasizing low taxation and efficiency rather than the provision of services to the needy.[17] Political theorists of a pluralist persuasion argue that the very idea of a public interest is a myth. Policy is, and should be, the result of the clash between the different interests and views which the contending groups which make up the public hold. Pluralists claim that any group which claims to advocate a policy 'in the public interest' is either deluded or more probably making propaganda. The pluralist objection to the possibility of there being any such thing as a public interest is probably ill founded. As Rousseau notes, though individuals or groups may start by advocating a selfish conception of their interests, if decision-making procedures are designed to block minority rule, ultimately agreement can be reached on a policy to the benefit of all, not that of a few, or even that of a simple majority.[18] Yet the critics of the city-manager movement were surely correct in their scepticism about whether or not an appointed official—or even an elected official—had a claim to represent the public interest.

It is even less plausible to suggest that a public interest group can make itself the guardian of the public interest. After all, Common Cause has a membership which is today less than half the population of a congressional district. Moreover, the membership of public interest groups is scarcely a representative sample of the population. It is common to note that public interest groups have a predominantly middle-class membership. MacFarland notes that in the early 1970s—before inflation made the figure less impressive—the average income of families belonging to Common Cause in Massachusetts was $20,000 and the subscription of $15 was enough to discourage less affluent families. In the League of Women Voters 68 per cent of the membership held college degrees; 50 per cent were married to professionals and 27 per cent to businessmen.[19] Apart from the middle-class character of their membership, public interest groups are accused of being concerned predominantly with issues of importance to the middle class. Labour lobbyists comment bitterly that Common Cause is silent on measures to combat poverty, advance social justice, and further civil rights, all issues on which unions have been active. It is frequently suggested that Common Cause's middle-class, often Republican, membership would resist any broader commitment to the causes which liberals favour. Consumer groups provide a useful service to those who can afford to buy new consumer goods, such as cars, but do nothing to increase the proportion of the population with the necessary money to buy these goods. Environmentalists concentrate their efforts on improving the appearance of the USA by protecting wilderness areas rather than by lobbying for urban renewal and the rebuilding of ghettoes. Conservatives point out that there are many legitimate goals which society might pursue—such as economic growth—which are given low priority by public interest groups. Even individual consumers may be willing to trade off some safety or reliability in exchange for cheaper products. Liberals make the same accusation with different examples; the abolition of poverty can be seen as just as much in the public interest as preserving Californian redwoods.

Such accusations do worry the public interest groups, if only for tactical reasons. Environmental groups have opened a dialogue with labour unions, and on some issues have formed a united front. For example, both environmentalists and the United Steelworkers have pressed for tighter controls on emissions from steel mills; the United Steelworkers argued quite plausibly that its members working in, or living near, the plants were the first to breathe in the pollution.[20] The consumer movement has also found co-operation with unions easy. The unions have a long history of consumer advocacy, and have always included consumer issues amongst the criteria they use for evaluating legislators. Only Common Cause has a reputation for arrogantly isolating itself and assuming an air of moral superiority *vis à vis* liberal groups and politicians. Yet even Common Cause does not make the extravagant claims to represent *the* public interest associated with the good-government movements of the early twentieth century. Whereas the good-government movement tried to take the politics out of government, Common Cause accepts that conflict over policy will continue; its role is merely to ensure that political debate will include reference to values which might be forgotten otherwise. As Gardner himself said

We don't want to take the politics out of politics. We don't want to take the special interests out of politics . . . We do feel very strongly that the special interests should operate openly, which means lobby disclosure, campaign finance disclosure. They should not use money in ways that corrupt the political process and there should be strong voices for the public interest in the battle.[21]

Common Cause's conception of politics is still pluralist, but pluralist processes must be reformed and a spokesman added for more general interests.

Public Interest Group Tactics

The fundamental advantage which public interest groups have enjoyed is that at first sight it is impossible to oppose their goals. Who can favour faulty and dangerous products, air pollution, corruption, and the despoliation of the environment? In fact, as we have noted, these are far from being the only conceivable goals of public policy. Even Common Cause's goals of more honest and efficient government may be regarded as secondary considerations. For example, liberal unions believed that Common Cause's plan to divide the House Education and Labor Committee in the interests of efficiency would have inhibited the passing of liberal education and welfare legislation. Yet public interest groups—unlike unions—do start with the inestimable advantage of advocating policies designed to achieve goals which in theory society in general favours.

Because of this advantage, public interest groups have placed considerable emphasis on research and publicity, bringing to light practices such as faulty car design or attempts to buy government decisions with campaign contributions. At its simplest, the strategy is exemplified by the League of Women Voters' exemplary efforts to increase the awareness of voters by arranging debates—often televised—between major candidates at state and federal level. At the other extreme is the research effort which Common Cause makes to analyse the source and destination of campaign contributions, an effort which has made the interest group the standard source of information on the subject. Common Cause also generates much of the information available on the inequities of the federal tax system. Environmental groups also need to spend a major part of their resources discovering the real risks involved in the use of such diverse inventions as atomic power stations and chemical fertilizers. Though public interest groups of course have to compete with corporations and government agencies able to spend far more on research to support their views, these groups have frequently established a high reputation for the quality of their work. In spite of its misfortunes with Congress Watch, the Nader organization is well regarded as a source of information, and Senator Ribicoff has noted that 'public interest groups produce sufficiently interesting work that you have practically every committee in Congress giving equal time to public interest people.'[22]

Research on its own is not enough. Public interest groups need ways in which they can make it clear to politicians who prefer vice to virtue that their sins have not passed unnoticed. Nearly all the public interest groups employ lobbyists whose task it is to present their organizations to Congress. Most of these lobbyists have a high reputation, and a few are amongst the best in their profession. David Cohen of Common Cause was paid over $40,000 a year in the late 1970s, and was thought to be worth his salary. Cohen also illustrates the personnel links between interest groups in Washington; whereas he used to be a labour lobbyist but moved to Common Cause, his predecessor left Common Cause to work for the United Auto Workers. In lobbying for their objectives public interest groups are helped enormously by the characteristics of their memberships. Most public interest group members are, like members of other interest groups, inactive. But the proportion who are active is unusually high. The ability of public interest groups to persuade members to spend time and money telephoning legislators or writing to them to urge a vote in line with the interest group's wishes, and checking afterwards to see how the legislator in fact acted, is unusually high. People who join public interest groups have an unusually high interest in at least an aspect of public policy; this represents a great strategic resource for public interest groups.

Thus the characteristics of public interest group members enable them to make an impact far in excess of what one would predict from their numbers.

Public interest groups have mastered the art of good press relations. Apart from the intrinsic interest of the stories which the public interest groups generate, the major organizations such as Common Cause have good links with reporters. Common Cause issues press releases in the form beginning 'A Common Cause study released today shows that . . ', which makes it easy for reporters or editors to print the material with minimal rewriting. Common Cause's Washington headquarters is in the same street as the television companies.

Public interest groups have also been effective and assiduous users of the courts to further their objectives. Mention has been made already of how Common Cause forced disclosure of contributions to the Nixon Committee to Re-Elect the President. The environmental and consumer groups have been equally ready to go to court. It is not entirely clear why public interest groups have placed such reliance on the courts. Of course, litigation involves the use of professionals—lawyers and expert witnesses— who are frequently willing to provide their services to such organizations at a lower cost than they would to other concerns. Perhaps the major explanation lies in the character of the recent legislation which Congress has adopted on environmental, worker, and consumer protection. Partly because of an inability to resolve the technical issues in legislation, and partly in order to reduce the political pressure on such issues, Congress has adopted broad legislation which gives regulatory agencies a very imprecisely drawn mandate to tackle a problem. In one extreme instance, the Environmental Protection Agency (EPA) was mandated to clean up water pollution without regard to cost by issuing suitable regulations. Of course, such an instruction taken at face value was ludicrous; the United States could devote its entire national income to tackling water pollution. However, the language of the act left much scope for the environmental groups to take the EPA to court alleging that the agency was not meeting the goals Congress had set it. Such lawsuits served not only to stiffen the terms of a particular regulation which was being contested but to exert pressure on the agency to frame stiffer regulations in the future lest it be taken to court again. Until recently, business has been slow to contest the detailed regulations formed under such acts unless a particular corporation has been forced to defend itself. As in several other spheres of political action, business was temporarily out-manoeuvred by public interest groups in the political use of courts.

A question which is asked increasingly, however, particularly as business becomes more sophisticated politically, is whether public interest groups have enough political clout. After a decade in which publicizing abuses and lobbying for their correction seemed enough, a number of commentators have suggested that groups such as the Nader organizations are weakened seriously by the absence of a capacity to mobilize voters or make campaign contributions on the lines of the AFL-CIO's COPE. Others have suggested that the public interest groups are finding that they need to work more closely with sympathetic groups outside the public interest fraternity. Indeed, there seems to have been a tendency for the public interest groups to be 'politicized'. The Nader organizations have found that many of their objectives can be achieved only through legislation, legislation which was often blocked by President Ford's vetoes of consumer legislation.[23] Partly because of these vetoes, though Nader did not endorse Carter formally in the 1976 election, the two are very closely associated. After his victory, Carter included Nader on the list of people to be consulted during the transition, and several of Nader's staff were given important political positions in the new administration.

The Nader organizations and the consumer movement in general frequently form coalitions with other interest groups, especially with organized labour, an unsuccessful example being the campaign for a consumer-advocacy agency in 1978. Environmentalists too are willing to form such coalitions which bring the public interest groups the advantage of organized labour's incomparably stronger political machine. Common Cause tends to remain aloof, preferring in its own view to call the issues as it sees them and, in the view of its critics behaving with typical arrogance. It is perhaps relevant that as one of the public interest groups with the largest and most active membership, and one which it is also hard to characterize ideologically, Common Cause has less to gain by allying with the older liberal interest groups such as organized labour. The current resurgence of the right in American politics, and the increased activism of business has strengthened the tendency for liberal unions and most of the public interest groups to work together. One restraint on public interest groups however, is the possibility that a highly aggressive or partisan approach will lead to the withdrawal of the tax-exempt status which most public interest groups claim. This tax-exempt status is of great importance to public interest group contributors as they can set their contributions against income tax under section 501 (c) (3) of the tax code. Yet this tax relief can be granted only if the Internal Revenue Service agrees that the public interest group in question is performing educational or charitable work. Particularly during the Nixon Administration withdrawal of 501 (c) (3) status was used as a weapon against public interest groups the Administration disliked, such as the Sierra Club, the National Resources Defence Council, and the Center for Corporate Responsibility. The larger groups, such as the Sierra Club, were able to survive by switching their lobbying activities to a nominally separate political organization. However, the Center for Corporate Responsibility was badly damaged by the IRS ruling. In general the fear of losing 501 (c) (3) status is a significant restraint on public interest groups, discouraging all but the largest from behaving too 'politically', i.e. lobbying or campaigning in a manner which upsets politicians.

Consequences for the System

What difference has the resurgence of public interest groups made to American politics? Some politicians believe that the answer is that they have made a great deal of difference. Representative Mikva (D., Illinois) has said that the rise of public interest groups is the most significant change that has happened during his service in Congress.[24] Those who dismiss the public interest groups as middle-class reformers are less sure; to New Deal liberals, most public interest groups devote their energies to the less important goals, neglecting the redistributive issues which to them are at the heart of politics. One dismissive comment often made about public interest groups is that they constitute no radical challenge to the system. If consumer groups succeed in imposing more stringent safety features on auto manufacturers, the auto manufacturers have nothing to fear; all manufacturers will simply charge more for their products to cover the cost. The cost of environmental and consumer-protection regulations, because they apply to all manufacturers, can be passed on to the consumer. In fact it is not clear that the costs of regulations will always fall equally on all manufacturers. Some cars, for example, are harder to redesign to meet safety requirements than others. Domestic steel producers have to compete with imports from Japan, where the government is less concerned about the health of its subjects. If radicals have been dismissive about public interest groups, businessmen are not. The emergence of public interest groups has done more than any other factor to stimulate political action by business in the United States.[25] The more astute businessmen know that public interest groups, as one businessman put it in an interview, 'are not a threat to business [i.e. capitalism] but are a threat to the *way* in which we are used to doing business.' The consumer and environmental interest groups have an uncertain effect on economic growth and profits; the regulations they have prompted government to issue have certainly placed corporations in a much more difficult legal position, limiting their freedom of action and leading to a major increase in the number of lawyers corporations employ. Common Cause is concerned with different kinds of policy. Yet it too has surely made an impact. Without the work that Common Cause did, not only to mobilize public opinion but also to produce coherent, workable plans for reform, the public's demand for changes after Watergate might have been dissipated, producing no more permanent results than did the demand for gun control after the assassination of President Kennedy. Instead, campaign-finance disclosure, federal financing of elections, and changes in Congress, such as departures from the seniority system which Common Cause has advocated, have given the American people a greater opportunity to influence public policy than they have enjoyed for many years.

Public interest groups have set out to provide a powerful voice for issues which concern everyone, but previously had lacked spokesmen in the interest group system. They have not plugged all of the gaps in pluralism; nor have they tried to. For example, the major public interest groups do nothing to provide the poor with a louder voice. Yet capitalizing on public moods which they alone could not have created—demands for more honest government, safer goods, and less pollution—public interest groups placed a new set of issues at the centre of the public agenda. Under their pressure, government has enacted regulations which have already produced a demonstrable improvement in car safety, the cleanliness of water, and increased efforts to reduce the presence in the environment of substances causing great human misery through diseases such as cancer. These are very worthwhile achievements.

Yet there was always something a little unreal about the success which public interest groups enjoyed. Some changes in American public policy take place after such a clear trial of strength that the change in policy clearly marks a permanent and significant change in the balance of political forces. Such major changes in public policy take place after sharp conflict between contending ideologies, parties, and interest groups; they usually take a major electoral victory. The changes in the role of government which we associate with the New Deal and the Great Society were such changes which it was impossible to reverse. No one could demolish the Social Security system or, after the adoption of Medicare, remove the federal government from the role of financing health care for a significant number of Americans. In contrast, the victories won by the consumer protection and environmental groups have resulted from no such comprehensive trial of strength. Indeed, the case which business might have mounted against the consumer or environmental groups went, if not by default, then clearly without business mobilizing its full resources. For example, in its struggle with Ralph Nader in 1966–7, General Motors had no permanent Washington representative. Its case was put primarily by middle-ranking managers flown in from Detroit—the company headquarters—for limited periods. General Motors did hire a firm of Washington lawyers to represent it, but with almost as much stupidity as in their decision to hire private detectives to shadow Nader, the law firm was instructed to make no compromises. Neither large corporations nor general business organizations would be so unprepared today. In short, some of the most important victories won by public interest groups were won before the business opponents of such groups were fully mobilized. As we have seen in our chapter on business and politics, the position is far different today.

Many of the public interest groups were likely to suffer a reduction in their power if, as has happened, groups whose interests their proposals disadvantaged—primarily business— began to realize their political potential. The United States had not made, in fact, an irreversible commitment to environ- mentalism or consumerism at almost any cost; the strength of public interest groups in the late 1960s and early 1970s was somewhat illusory. However, a number of other factors have further weakened the public interest groups. First, membership has stagnated and even declined. Common Cause was forced to make major budget cuts after a fall of 100,000 (almost a third) in its membership between 1974 and 1978. Second, partly because of this fall in membership, public interest groups have lost momentum and prestige. Public interest groups are not ignored, but they are increasingly treated as but one part of the political scene. Competition between the large number of public interest groups has weakened the illusion that any one of them speaks for *the* public interest. Such conflicts—for example between the Sierra Club and Friends of the Earth—remind politicians that no one public interest group is likely to have the only defensible attitude or policy, and that public interest groups advocate but one possible viewpoint amongst many. More practically, competition between the mushrooming number of such groups has reduced the yield of appeals to the public for funds. 'Direct mail' appeals are producing so little money for public interest groups that their viability is questionable. The feeling that there is nothing special about public interest groups has been strengthened by the belief amongst politicians that they often play a familiar kind of politics. Thus the 'Dirty Dozen' list of Representatives with the 'worst' voting record on environmental issues has clearly been manipulated to put the House Republican Leader, John Rhodes, on the list and to keep others off.[26]

Beyond all this, the climate of opinion has turned against public interest groups in a less tangible way. It is much easier today to criticize groups such as Common Cause for producing unwelcome and unanticipated changes in government than it used to be—one example being the increased opportunities for lobbyists its 'sunshine' laws, requiring open committee meetings in Congress, produced. Above all, the mood is much less indulgent towards environmentalists and consumer groups. When in March 1979 Judge John Sirica, the hero of the Watergate cases, ruled that he would not recognize the Nader organizations in his court as spokesmen for the public interest on the grounds that they had no machinery by which Nader might be removed from the leadership by members and hence were undemocratic, his ruling was greeted with much amusement and little criticism. The liberal Rural Electrification Association ran adverts in liberal magazines such as the *New Republic* arguing that environmental regulation had reached a ludicrous level; whereas it used to be necessary to obtain six federal permits to build a power station, the number could now be sixty-four. A successful lawsuit to block construction of a hydro-electric dam because the construction would endanger a species on the EPA's list of endangered species, the snail darter, made the Endangered Species Act itself endangered; to conciliate Congress, the EPA reduced its list of endangered species drastically. Above all, as real incomes stagnated in the 1970s and inflation and unemployment continued at postwar record levels, the willingness of the public to sacrifice material prosperity to the goals of public interest groups diminished. Even those well disposed to the environmental movement have been given cause to pause by estimates that the cost of environmental controls are projected to rise from $19 billion to $51 billion between 1979 and 1986.[27] Public interest groups enjoyed their fastest rate of growth in the early 1970s at the end of thirty years of almost unbroken economic growth. In 1970, whatever the other problems of the United States, constantly increasing economic prosperity could be taken for granted. Now it cannot. Public interest groups whose goals imply a slower rate of economic growth have suffered inevitably.

Yet if public interest groups have suffered a decline in their influence, they have not been routed. Memberships, income, and influence have stabilized at a significant level, even if lower than in the early 1970s. Public interest groups show every sign of continuing to advocate effectively a safer, cleaner America ruled by more honest politicians. The relevance of this to our central argument is obvious. Important policy considerations which twenty years ago often went unconsidered now have effective organizations to raise them. The range of issues included in the interest-group system has once again increased.

More Views of the Public Interest

The well-known public interest groups have functioned as forerunners for a new wave of highly publicized 'single issue groups'. Of course, single issue groups are by no means a new phenomenon in American history and are hard to distinguish analytically from the public interest groups; single issue groups often pursue unselfish goals, and, like Common Cause or the Nader groups, believe that their policies are for the public good. Frequently a vehicle for right-wing politics, the single issue groups are heirs to a tradition including the Grand Army of the Republic (a very selfish single issue group of Civil War veterans seeking higher pensions), the pro-Chiang Kai-Chek 'Committee of a Million', and the National Rifle Association, a group opposed to gun control which remains the most permanent and powerful of the single issue groups, though over a hundred years old. Popular magazines such as *Newsweek* or *Time* have run features discussing the effects on political life of groups which are prepared to commit funds or votes for or against a candidate solely on the basis of his or her vote for one particular issue. How in view of the existence of earlier examples of single issue groups, can commentators take seriously the idea that single interest groups are a new force?

The answer takes us back to the similarities in the circumstances which have helped both single interest groups, and public interest groups. As we have noted, the American public shows an unwillingness to participate in political parties or to follow them loyally. Instead, the political activists have looked for opportunities to influence politics outside the parties and the public is more responsive to issues. The vulnerability of politicians to pressure-group activity has increased too. Candidates for office, unable to obtain enough money, organization, or votes for victory from the parties, look for all these components of political success, particularly money and organization, from interest groups. Over the last thirty years a variety of interest groups, including labour, business, and a number of public or single interest groups, have improved their political organization and capacity to raise money while the parties have languished. Reforms such as an increase in the number of recorded votes in Congress and open Committee meetings make it easier to monitor the views of Congressmen on each issue. Technological changes such as computerized mailing lists and WATS telephone lines make the formation of mass membership organizations for limited purposes easier. Single issue and public interest groups have flourished for the same reasons.

Single issue groups can be divided into at least two types. First, there are those that handle issues which though they may cut across political parties are issues of general concern at the centre of political debate. A notable example was the formation of single issue groups both to support and to oppose ratification of the Panama Canal Treaties in 1978. Second, there are single issue groups which exist to handle specialized issues such as gun control or abortion which without the existence of the groups would be minor footnotes to political life.

The formation of single issue groups to work on important political issues is a technique which has a particular appeal to the right wing because the alternative to interest-group activity, the Republican Party, is so weak. One of the main pioneers and practitioners of interest-group activity, Richard Viguerie, has argued that conservatives are ill advised to associate themselves with the Republican Party because the Republican Party label repels far more people than it attracts; after all, only some 22 per cent of the population identify with the Republican Party. Viguerie believes that the computerized mailing lists which he has amassed, containing the lists of all known to have supported conservative causes in the past, provide conservative causes and candidates with a better chance of success than relying on the crumbling Republican Party. Viguerie has certainly demonstrated an awesome capacity to raise funds for conservative candidates such as Senator Thurmond (R., South Carolina). On the other hand, the costs of such techniques are very high; almost two-thirds of receipts go to cover the costs of the appeal for funds.

Many criticisms are made of single issue groups. Politicians object to being judged on the basis of a single vote. Commentators fear that the task of creating a majority for each proposal is made more difficult; tactics for coalition building such as logrolling and bargaining, which assume the existence of legislators indifferent on a particular issue, are precluded as each item on the political agenda becomes hotly contested. Others object that the tiny public interest groups can have disproportionate influence because of their single-minded readiness to commit money and votes against their opponents on a single issue. As pluralist defenders of the status quo have always argued that one of the virtues of the American political system was the ability it gave to minorities with intense feelings to affect public policy, such complaints from the political establishment are ironic. Yet both critics of, and apologists for, single issue groups assume that they are effective.

In fact, the evidence suggests that single issue groups can make only a marginal difference. This is partly because it is rare for there to be a single issue group on only one side of the issue. Thus the abortion issue has produced an intense conflict between the anti-abortionists, the so-called 'right to life' movement, and the feminists and 'pro-choice' groups. The 'pro-life' groups (which do not include opposition to the death penalty or war amongst their goals) appear to be more influential because the issue is in fact moot. The Supreme Court—the Court whose majority was supposedly conservative after President Nixon's appointments, has discovered a constitutional right to abortion during the first three months of pregnancy and a qualified right to abortion in the next three months. Thus politicians feeling pressure on the issue can yield to the anti-abortion groups knowing that nothing can be done to outlaw abortion. The anti-abortion groups claimed a major role in the defeat of Senator Clark (D., Iowa) in 1978. Yet spokesmen for such groups claimed to have delivered only 25,000 votes to Clark's opponent, a fraction of his total vote.

Probably the most plausibly powerful single issue group is the National Rifle Association (NRA). Founded in 1871 to promote more accurate marksmanship and helped ever since by the rifle manufacturers and the government, the NRA has intransigently and successfully opposed any effective gun control. In spite of the assassinations of President Kennedy, Robert Kennedy, and Martin Luther King, there are practically no federal regulations on who can buy guns, and fewer than ten states have such laws. (The view that gun control is barred by the constitution is in fact fallacious.) As the NRA has a budget of $17 million (of which $4 million is spent on lobbying activities) it is easy to see why. The NRA has claimed the 'credit' for the elimination at the polls of such advocates of gun control as Senators Gore (D., Tenn.), Goodell (R., New York), Dodd (D., Connecticut), and Tydings (D., Maryland). The NRA made a particular effort to eliminate Tydings, producing half a million brochures against him and paying for numerous commercials against him. Yet, as Sherrill notes,[28] it is hard to take all of these claims—or perhaps any of them—seriously. Other factors affected every race. Goodell was on the Nixon Administration's 'hit' list and faced both a Democrat and a Conservative opponent; Dodd had been censured by the Senate for misconduct and Tydings was badly smeared by an inaccurate *Life* magazine article. Many other Senators who have incurred the wrath of the NRA have survived and candidates such as Richard Hughes, when he ran for the Governorship of New Jersey, have done very well after bitter attacks from the NRA.

The NRA also suffers from an image of being part of the far or lunatic right wing. Some 25 per cent of its members do not even shoot, but join merely to support the right to bear arms; NRA spokesmen cater to such generally conservative members. Yet partly because of the odd character of much of its membership, the NRA can produce floods of mail. This mail will have little effect on some politicians. Thus President Johnson was not moved by receiving 2,000 letters from NRA members, nor Senator Edward Kennedy by even more letters, about the Vietnam war. However, as writers such as Fenno have noted, politicians vary considerably in the way in which they react to pressure.[29] Some are panicked by a very limited amount of pressure. Above all, though the NRA may have less power than is commonly supposed, there are in the background some 60 million Americans who own guns, and whose votes are a greater deterrent than the NRA from supporting gun-control legislation.

Our scepticism about the power of the NRA suggests that the alleged danger of single issue groups should not be exaggerated. The NRA has funds and a large membership, which none of the recent single issue groups has been able to achieve. If it is so uncertain that the NRA is as powerful as its officers would portray it, the newer, smaller groups are unlikely to fare better. Yet this is not to argue that the single issue groups are of no consequence. As the history of the NRA suggests—even if its critics are right—a group's reputation for being powerful may far outrun its real potential. Just as many politicians—*pace* Sherrill—think that the NRA is powerful, so newer single issue groups attract attention in Washington in spite of having a limited capacity to deliver either votes or money to a candidate. Moreover, single issue groups do seem to have provided not so much a new, as a more frequently travelled, road for those who wish to be actively involved in politics. The increase in the number and importance of economic interest groups which we have noted so often has been paralleled by a similar increase in the number and importance of non-economic, single issue groups. A large number of groups now speak on a wider range of issues.

Lobbying and Lobbyists

The preceding chapters have shown that there has been a major change in the extent to which the different interests in society are involved in politics. We might ask, however, whether this change in the range of interests actively seeking to influence decision takers has been accompanied by a change in the manner in which interest groups seek to shape government policy. There are grounds for believing that in fact pressure-group techniques have changed, and that pressure-group practices today are both more open, and more vigorous than in the past. In order to substantiate this claim it is necessary to describe the world of the lobbyist of the 1950s as encapsulated in the literature, and then to suggest ways in which the situation has changed.

The Conventional Picture

According to the established literature, the American public had little to fear from lobbyists, and possibly much to be grateful for. The same could be said, almost *a fortiori*, for the legislators and officials who dealt with lobbyists. By and large, lobbying was, to use Milbrath's phrase, a communications process.[1] Rather than lobbyists exerting pressure or exercising a malevolent influence on public policy through bribery and corruption, they were at their best suppliers of technical information which enabled better policy to be made. Lobbyists became in effect unpaid staff members for legislators, sometimes on such close terms with legislators that the lobbyists began to see problems too much from the perspective of the legislator, and too little from that of his members. It is worth spelling out why the lobbyists were thought to possess such limited power. The reasons given in studies of lobbyists covered the nature of the electorate and of Congress as well as the lobbyists themselves.

The American electorate in the 1950s was one which was highly unsuited to the exercise of pressure-group power. According to that classic of the voting-behaviour literature, the *American Voter*,[2] the public was little influenced by issues or the candidates' positions on the issues in deciding how to vote. Indeed, voters were unable to place parties, let alone individual candidates, on the side of a political controversy which they actually took. Instead voters were guided by a feeling of loyalty to a political party, party identification, which was learnt from parents at an early age and not abandoned in spite of changes in the social class or political principles of the individual. Pressure groups which seek to influence the way in which their members vote—or even the votes of members of the public at large— always face the difficulty that what to the pressure group may be *the* issue of a campaign may be comparatively inconsequential to their members, let alone to the public. The electorate described by the authors of the *American Voter* was unlikely to be swayed even by an issue the voters agreed was important. Only the farming community stood out from this somewhat depressing picture. Farmers and their families displayed considerable volatility, switching their support between the parties to a considerable degree from election to election and showing a willingness to vote on the basis of one issue alone—farm prices. This interesting way in which farmers differed from the public in general probably reflects the vigorous debate between Republicans and Democrats on farm policy since 1928.

It is understandable, therefore, that V. O. Key[3] should have concluded that pressure groups had no power to impose electoral sanctions on politicians. Indeed, Key argued that only rash lobbyists would threaten a legislator with electoral reprisals, and that when they did so, they were threatening politicians with an empty gun.[4] By and large it was understandable that lobbyists should seek a close and trusting relationship with politicians; after all, they were powerless to coerce politicians. There were some exceptions. The American Medical Association worked hard to defeat advocates of 'socialized medicine' or even Medicare. More significantly, the AFL-CIO made contributions in cash and kind to candidates it favoured, and vociferously advocated the defeat of legislators who, in its view, had the worst voting records in Congress. Yet the exceptions proved the rule. Most commentators concluded that the role of the AMA in defeating advocates of Medicare was greatly exaggerated.[5] Studies of the impact of that most politically active of unions, the United Auto Workers, in areas where its strength was greatest seemed to show that, even under favourable circumstances, the capacity of unions to deliver their members' votes was minimal,[6] a conclusion which some had expected since the President of the UMW, John L. Lewis, had failed conspicuously to persuade his members to vote for Wilkie in 1940 to save the country from the supposed tyranny of Roosevelt (and increase the importance of John L. Lewis). If unions, at that time by far the biggest and most organized of the pressure groups spending money on politics, seemed to have as little effect as Kornhauser *et al.* showed in their study of the UAW, then other interest groups would do well to avoid electoral action.

Several characteristics of the Congress seemed also to weaken the power of lobbyists. The most powerful places in that body were occupied by those who had the least to fear electorally. After the Democrats regained control of Congress in 1954, fully three-fifths of the powerful Committee chairmanships were held by Southern Democrats who were typically almost immune from electoral defeat. The flow of legislation through the House of Representatives was controlled by a Rules Committee dominated by a conservative coalition of Southern Democrats and rural Republicans almost equally secure in retaining office as long as they wished. Both Committee chairmen and the Rules Committee would from time to time 'take the heat' for their colleagues by accepting responsibility for blocking legislation favoured by interest groups.[7]

Most of the studies of the Congress of the 1950s emphasized additional techniques which the legislator could use to avoid unwelcome pressure from interest groups. Many of these turned on adroit use of Congressional procedure. Rather than oppose an interest group publicly, thus encouraging retaliation, legislators could have a 'voice vote' in which the position of each individual would not be recorded. Legislators could vote for a general position favoured by interest groups, but could support amendments undermining the bill. Legislators could acquiesce in the adoption of conference-committee reports which were worded in such a way that they effectively sabotaged the bill they supposedly approved. Moreover, legislators could drop hints to lobbyists, if they were needed, that even if they were voting against an interest group on this issue, they might vote as it wished on a subsequent issue. Moreover, most legislators voting on any given issue would not have a constituency interest involved. Most Representatives do not have a large proportion of their electors who are farmers, union members, or businessmen. Rarely was there a constituency interest or attitude which was so strong that the Representative had to bow before it; indeed, Miller and Stokes found a close fit between constituency opinion and the Representative's voting record only on civil-rights issues.[8]

The opportunities for legislators to follow their own opinion, and not interest-group pressure, were increased by the apparently low level of competence amongst lobbyists in the 1950s. In their massive study of trade policy in the 1950s Bauer, Pool, and Dexter[9] reported that interest-group officials were highly regarded neither by legislators nor by people they represented. Businessmen apparently regarded officials of trade associations as people who were incapable of functioning as businessmen. Legislators felt that interest-group officials maintained contact only with Representatives and Senators who were already on their side. Moreover, trade associations typically disposed of few resources to spend on research or propaganda. Indeed, the typical trade association spent more energy on maintaining its own structure and membership than on coercing politicians. One of the main themes of Bauer, Pool, and Dexter's book was that there are often interest groups on both sides of an issue. However, though that is often true (as when the AFL-CIO and AMA opposed each other on Medicare) Bauer, Pool, and Dexter also emphasized the surprising weakness of the groups involved in such conflicts.

The stereotype notion of omnipotent groups becomes completely untenable once there are groups aligned on both sides. The result of opposing equipotent forces is stalemate. But even taken by themselves the groups did not appear to have the raw material of great power.[10]

Many interest groups did not maintain any permanent lobbying organization in Washington. Large corporations such as General Motors and, until 1961, ITT, entrusted their affairs to Washington law firms such as Covington and Burling which specialize in political work. Though the Washington lawyers might go into court to defend their clients (e.g. against an anti-trust action) or appear before a Regulatory Commission considering an order against the clients, the role of the Washington lawyers went much wider.[11] Their role was to represent clients before all branches of government including Congress and the Executive as well as the Judiciary. Very often knowledge of Washington personalities, of whom to approach, and how, on any issue, was far more important than knowledge of the law. In an era in which many of business's critics were without a coherent voice (e.g. before the advent of effective public interest groups), the Washington law firms with their knowledge of which levers to pull on issues were all that even a large corporation needed. Though the Washington law firms flourish today (obviously benefiting from the increase in the number of regulations), they are no longer considered sufficient by corporations to defend their interests. Until recently, however, most lobbyists in Washington have been surprisingly poorly linked to the Executive branch, and it is this gap that the law firms have been particularly astute at filling.

Faced with so many limitations on his power, the lobbyist of the 1950s, as portrayed in the established literature, came to rely on developing a close, trusting relationship with the politician. It is interesting to recall the attributes which the lobbyists and politicians interviewed by Milbrath regarded as being hallmarks of a good lobbyist. The picture which emerges of the lobbyist at his best is one of a person who is more helpful than coercive. The lobbyist should be honest and have a strong sense of integrity, including regard for the public interest. It was essential that the lobbyist be capable and well informed. The lobbyist 'is basically dependent on the actions of others' and must therefore be agreeable. The lobbyist must be able to express his ideas well, and in a persuasive fashion. He must also be persistent. One of Milbrath's respondents summarized these expectations of what a lobbyist should be by saying: 'If over a period of time you do not let anybody down and you have been faithful and constructively worked for the cause of your people then the members of Congress will have confidence in you and put themselves in your hands. That should be one of the highest aims of a lobbyist.'[12]

How accurately the accounts of lobbying in the 1950s described interest-group politics can be questioned. Understandable research problems as well as the somewhat complacent attitudes of the 1950s about government may well have distorted the true picture. For example, Milbrath's survey of lobbyists covered a sample of those who had registered with Congress as lobbyists. These people were known to be a small percentage of lobbyists in Washington. Because the definition of lobbying used in the 1947 Act regulating lobbying was so narrow, employees of such well-known lobbies as the National Association of Manufacturers or Chamber of Commerce did not bother to register. Moreover, in an era in which there were no real counterparts to the Congressional hearings on Watergate, the ITT and Chile, the ITT's pressure on the anti-trust division of the Justice Department nor any White House tapes, the seamy side of politics was not so obvious. Unfortunately, this lack of evidence caused many writers on interest groups to assume that corruption and other underhand techniques had largely vanished from American national (if not State) politics. It is easy to see how these biases developed. The political scientists such as Milbrath had to work from some list of lobbyists which was already available. Political scientists lacked the investigative resources which Congressional committees were to deploy in the 1970s to reveal some of the underhand techniques in use in politics. But we should bear in mind the probability that the somewhat complacent writers on interest groups of twenty years ago were unaware of important aspects of lobbying and interest-group politics.

In some respects, too, the literature of the 1950s may have understated the effectiveness of interest groups. It was a common complaint of the legislators Bauer, Pool, and Dexter interviewed that lobbyists contacted only legislators already likely to agree with their case. Bauer, Pool, and Dexter treated this complaint seriously. In fact, such a strategy may not have been unwise. All the studies of lobbying agree that the best lobbyist of a Representative is a Representative (and *mutatis mutandis* the same is true for Senators.) In fact many interests, including large corporations and unions, have their favourite legislators, often from the area where that interest is based itself. It is often better for lobbyists to brief a sympathetic legislator and leave him or her to approach colleagues than for the lobbyist to approach unknown legislators directly. On some occasions, friendly legislators would be on the Committees of most concern to the interest group anyway. Thus Democrats on the Agriculture Committee and the Education and Labor Committee were in any case the best placed to help respectively the National Farmers' Union and the AFL-CIO.

Changes in Lobbying

The lobbyist of the 1950s would not be surprised by many features of lobbying in the 1980s. He might, however, notice some important changes which, without introducing wholly new techniques into lobbying, have altered the balance between the techniques used. First, however, let us mention some features of the lobbyist's life and work which are much the same. For example, lobbyists still attach great importance to maintaining close links with government officials. An official working for ITT wrote:

There are several executive departments which are important to ITT and therefore contacts have to be maintained . . . I spend at least two nights a week with government personnel. These evenings include socialising, arranging and attending parties, attending sports events and other functions. Weekends are usually spent with Hill personnel.[13]

Such meetings are probably not the occasion for much detailed talking. When Dita Beard, the ITT lobbyist, tried to make use of a reception given by Governor Nunn on the day of the Kentucky Derby, her well-lubricated comments were very embarrassing, doing more harm than good to the cause of stopping the anti-trust action against ITT.[14] However, such meetings do create an atmosphere of trust and *bonhomie* which are of help to the company. The social contacts established at such meetings may also serve a political purpose; ITT was able to put its case against the Justice Department's anti-trust suit to almost every top figure in the Nixon Administration, no doubt partly through the social ties forged by ITT lobbyists.

A second feature of the relationship between lobbyists and legislators which remains the same is that legislators need and appreciate technical guidance from lobbyists. Eloquent testimony that legislators need this help has come from the somewhat unexpected source of Senator Metcalf, who is a liberal Democrat.

I want to say to you that as one legislator for almost three decades now, that I use the services of lobbyists in my activities more than lobbyists come and see me. One of my favorite lobbyists is the Montana Power Co. I do not think that anyone would say I am subservient to the Montana Power Co., but when I want some information I go [to] the Montana Power Co.'s lobbyist who is here in Washington and ask him if he could find it out for me. With all justice, they have never given me false information. Another favorite lobbyist of mine is the Anaconda Copper Mining Co. Every time I go to the Anaconda Copper Mining people for information, they give me the information I desire.[15]

Somewhat later in the same hearing, Senator Metcalf, who was no tool of the special interests, commented, 'I just do not know how any of us would function in this very complicated area we are in without the activities of the various lobbying organisations.' It is worth noting, however, that the two examples which sprang to Metcalf's mind were of individual companies, not trade associations, supplying information suggesting that in this respect, too, the work had not changed drastically since Bauer, Pool, and Dexter wrote.

The major changes in the methods of pressure-group politics in the last ten years have been the frequent and open use of methods amounting to pressure rather than mere persuasion. Duverger argued that political parties were affected by a contagion from the left in which more right-wing, conservative parties gradually adopted the techniques employed by their more left-wing competitors.[16] Though Duverger's thesis has declined in popularity, it has much validity if applied to American pressure groups. Many of the techniques pioneered by unions and public interest groups have been refined and extended more recently by business and professional groups.

One of the most obvious examples is the growth of financial involvement by interest groups in openly raising funds for election campaigns. The relationship between money and elections in the United States has been longstanding and warm. Both liberal and conservative candidates have benefited from family fortunes or large gifts from friends. (One of the more interesting of recent examples was that of Senator George McGovern, whose quest for the 1972 Democratic nomination was helped to gather impetus by the generosity of the Xerox heir's contributions to the Senator's campaign.) The systematic gathering of funds to aid sympathetic candidates was pioneered by the labour unions. Almost from their foundation, the CIO unions had made political contributions. The creation of the AFL-CIO in 1955 made possible the more co-ordinated giving of campaign contributions by unions, while the passing of the 'anti-union' Taft–Hartley Act in 1947 made the unions more anxious to be involved effectively in politics. The AFL-CIO's Committee on Political Education (COPE) has carried evaluation of Candidates' voting records on a wide range of issues ever since its inception. The amount of money given by COPE and the individual unions has risen steadily ever since, so that by the early 1970s the unions were contributing over $8 million to political campaigns, and were by far the largest of the open contributors to politics.

The political contributions of business groups have only recently been made openly and honestly. Careful observers of political contributions have long known that though 18 US Code 610 forbids companies to make political contributions, many have long done so. Some of the reasons for these contributions, and the ways in which the law was evaded have been described in Chapter 4. In brief, the most popular techniques were for funds to be laundered by foreign subsidiaries, or for employees to make political contributions on behalf of their company, for which they were reimbursed with bogus merit bonuses from their employer. Such illicit practices became more prevalent throughout the 1960s and reached their climax in 1972 when the Committee to Re-Elect the President (CREEP) ran a systematic extortion racket demanding money with menaces from many of the best-known companies in the United States.

Subsequent legislation, particularly the 1974 Campaign Finances Act, cleared the way for open business involvement in Congressional elections (though the practice of providing public financing in Presidential elections more or less eliminated one major opportunity). Since 1974, the corporations have been entitled to form political action committees (PACs) which have all the costs of establishing and running them met from general company revenue. One business PAC, BIPAC, had existed since 1963 but had not flourished. Funds for disbursement to individual candidates are collected from shareholders, managers, and even—on two occasions per year when company and union PACs are allowed to collect funds from 'the other side'—from employees of the company. The widespread distribution of PAC funds from business to a variety of candidates (including liberal Democrats) has been discussed earlier in Chapter 4. However, our concern here is merely to point to the way in which business has copied unions, and indeed improved on their performance. Business PACs alone now make campaign contributions equivalent to those of the unions in combination with allied groups such as Real Estate and American Medical Association PACs. The total is much higher for business than for labour.

A similar tale can be told about the growth in the extent and quality of lobbying. As recently as the early 1960s, it was common for such major companies as General Motors and ITT to rely on Washington law firms for any representation they needed in federal policy making. Once again, the unions, and in particular the AFL-CIO, were regarded as possessing far larger and better lobbying staffs than any other interest. Of late the situation has changed. In the early 1970s the unions found that they had to compete for the title of most effective lobby with some highly competent public interest groups such as Common Cause; indeed, the unions found that they had to compete with the public interest groups for staff, too, as several top union lobbyists moved over to public interest groups. The conjunction of the closing of the illicit channels of business political influence and increased concern amongst the business community has prompted a rapid increase in the number and quality of business lobbyists. Apart from the rapid increase in the numbers of business representatives in Washington, the quality of business lobbying has been improved tremendously. Organizations such as the Chamber of Commerce, recently regarded as something of a joke by Washington *cognoscenti*, have emerged as the most sophisticated practitioners of the new lobbying techniques. In recent conflicts with the unions and public interest groups, business lobbyists have emerged as the victors, outmaneouvring their opponents regularly. The days when unions were much better equipped politically than business have passed; now unions recognize that they must learn from business the changed techniques of lobbying. Business lobbyists still attend seminars on effective political action at Common Cause, but they have less to learn than in the past.

It is ironic that business should have perfected many of the new lobbying strategies, for the new strategies are much more populist or participatory than the old. Most of the accounts of lobbying in the 1950s emphasized the value of trusting, technically informed links between lobbyist and politician. Manufactured waves of popular feeling, if detected as such, were regarded as vulgar and valueless exercises. Bauer, Pool, and Dexter found that some Representatives so heavily discounted mail stimulated by interest groups that they thought that they had received no mail on the subject at all.[17] Milbrath, too, found that 'members of Congress discount letter and telegram campaigns.'[18] Though lobbyists interviewed by Milbrath varied in their opinion of the utility of mail campaigns, with most rating the tactic poorly, nearly all of his Congressional respondents had a low opinion of the effectiveness of the tactic. Milbrath did emphasize that an argument telling a legislator about the effects of a programme on his constituency was valuable, though Bauer, Pool, and Dexter emphasized the practical difficulties legislators experience in discovering what their constituents' interests really are.

In line with general 'contagion from the left' which has changed the style of interest-group activity generally, the changes in lobbying activity were pioneered not by business but by the public interest groups and the anti-war movement. The anti-Vietnam War movement, building on the experience of the civil-rights campaigns, placed great stress on the use of demonstrations to attract attention and persuade. By the late 1970s, the most unlikely people were demonstrating in Washington, to the irritation of its inhabitants. The American Agriculture Movement brought a magnificent display of very expensive farm equipment to town while neatly attired supporters of nuclear power pressed leaflets on passers-by with a fervour more common in radical circles. As with many lobbying tactics, this taking to the streets was not always effective, but neither was it so doomed to failure as to be irrational. As the more left-wing groups had discovered, demonstrations not only displayed an intensity of feeling the politicians could not ignore but also brought the cause extensive (and free) publicity from the mass media. A demonstration in Washington is *de rigueur* for most movements today.

So are measures to involve members back in the districts and states. This technique was first developed systematically by Common Cause. As we have seen, one of the major advantages enjoyed by public interest groups is the middle-class nature of their membership, which renders it much more willing to engage in political activity than are the members of most interest groups. During campaigns to achieve Common Cause's major successes, such as the Campaign Finance Act of 1974, Common Cause members were encouraged to make Representatives and Senators aware of their existence. Whereas the more traditional form of lobbying assumed that approaches to legislators from the rank and file of the membership would be damaging because of the ignorance or insensitivity of the membership in arguing for a complicated bill, Common Cause was able to assume that its members had all the skills needed. Yet once the vogue for involving the ordinary members in lobbying had been developed by Common Cause (and speedily taken up by other public interest groups), other lobbies felt obliged to follow. In an era in which a high premium was placed on participation, older interest groups could not allow the public interest groups to claim exclusively the credit which went with involving the people in politics. By the late 1970s, unions were bringing ordinary workers to Washington to testify on the need to reform the labour-relations laws, and employers were responding by flying in literally thousands of small businessmen to lobby against labour-law reform and the creation of an agency to present the consumers' case to courts or regulatory agencies.

Even for business organizations, however, bringing the members to Washington is an expensive operation which can be mounted only occasionally. It is far cheaper to mobilize the membership back in the districts. Moreover, it has long been an adage of American interest groups (little exploited until the present) that legislators are far more worried about opinion in the district than about the views of national interest-group leaders. Building on the example of Common Cause, business groups have placed great emphasis on ensuring that their members back in the districts will lobby legislators effectively.

In part this is achieved by encouraging the formation of local political action committees which make contributions to election-campaign expenses. However, business groups are now moving out beyond this. In a step which is admired by other professionals (for example in the unions), the rejuvenated Chamber of Commerce has created Congressional Action Committees which will be the lobbying counterpart of Political Action Committees. In 1979 the research section of the Chamber of Commerce planned to provide local Chambers and their Congressional Action Committees with forecasts of the probable effect of proposed legislation on their locality within days of its consideration being announced. The Congressional Action Committees in their turn are expected to mobilize local business-men to telephone or write to their Representative and Senator in time to affect the outcome of the vote. Pilot studies conducted by the Chamber seem to have shown that this tactic can have a noticeable effect on a Representative's voting pattern. Of course, the Chamber of Commerce is hoping to prompt a flow of more informed and apparently more spontaneous mail to Washington than the old-fashioned form letters of the past. Nevertheless, it is interesting to notice how lobbying tactics, even those used by business groups, have changed in a more participatory manner.

It is possible that the trend towards more vigorous and open lobbying has gone too far, and has prompted Congressional resentment. In hearings on a bill (which came to nothing) to tighten lobbying regulations, Senator Brock pointed out that the Association of American Railroads had spent $1 million in support of one act (the Surface Transportation Act). Senator Ribicoff pointed out that 'The stream of letters or mailgrams we all receive may be a representative and spontaneous reflection of the public's view or it may only represent a secretly generated campaign by just one special interest. Congress and the public have a right to know . . .'[19] Common Cause has provided us with some amusing examples of how special interests tried to prompt a flow of apparently spontaneous mail. The American Trial Lawyers' Association was anxious to defeat a proposal in 1974 for 'no fault' insurance settlements for motorists' accident claims so that the expense of the parties taking each other to court (and hiring trial lawyers) would be avoided. The Trial Lawyers' Association arranged with the Western Union telegram company for mailgrams opposing the legislation to be sent to key Congressmen from Western Union offices around the country. Members of the Association could telephone the Western Union office, give the names of ten friends and associates, and for every name given, ten messages were sent to Congress. The association even arranged for Western Union's sales force to encourage local trial lawyers' associations to use the service. In the course of a campaign to prevent the Department of Health, Education and Welfare from insisting on the use of non-proprietary drugs (which are of course cheaper than name brands), the drug companies sought support from chemists and doctors. The salesmen of Ayerst Laboratories were ordered by the company to obtain letters opposing the plan from five chemists each. The letters would then be presented to the Secretary of HEW as proof of the opposition of the nation's chemists to his plan.[20]

Of course, the game of pretending that a manufactured outburst of feeling is spontaneous is one which has gone on for some time, and was familiar to writers such as Milbrath in the 1950s. The vast increase in the volume of lobbying and the money spent on it since the 1950s is hard to chart because of the numerous loop-holes in the 1946 Lobbying Disclosure Act. Congress could never prohibit, or even control, lobbying, as to do so would be construed as a breach of the Constitution's guarantees. Congress can, however, enact requirements for detailed lobbying disclosure which interest groups would dislike, partly because of the increased light they would cast on their affairs, and partly because meeting the requirements would impose a noticeable burden on the interest groups in terms of administrative costs. The threat of legislation, and the ill will engendered by obvious attempts at arm twisting may yet impose some limits on mass lobbying.

Lobbyists and the Executive

Most of the literature on lobbying in the United States focuses on contacts with Congress, not with the Executive. This tells us more about the comparative ease and difficulty of carrying out research on the Executive and Congress than about the balance struck by lobbyists. There is no doubt in the minds of practitioners that the Executive has become as important a focus for lobbyists as the Congress. Indeed, Congressional hearings on lobbying in 1975 produced much evidence that lobbying of the Executive branch is so frequent that it would cost companies and pressure groups an intolerable amount to record all contacts between their employees and government officials.[21] Pressure-group officials frequently remark on the rate at which the resources they devote to lobbying the Executive are increasing.

The reasons why more attention to the American Executive is required will be familiar to students of comparative politics, even though one could not argue seriously that Congress had suffered heavily in domestic affairs (or, in the 1970s, in foreign affairs) from the supposedly universal decline in the importance of legislatures. Much detailed work is delegated by Congress both to independent regulatory commissions and to agencies within the Executive branch. Though the decisions of such bodies can be, and frequently are, subject to appeal to the courts (on the grounds that their regulations do not accord with legislative intent) or to Congress in the form of requests to reverse the decision of a regulatory agency by fresh legislation (such as an amendment to an appropriations bill), it saves a great deal of trouble to reach an agreement with the regulatory agency itself. In recent years the number of agencies affecting industry has risen considerably. The Environmental Protection Agency (EPA) and the Occupational Safety and Health Administration (OSHA) have been particularly important in prompting an upsurge of pressure-group interest in the Executive. Both agencies issue and enforce rules which balance public safety against commercial advantage, mobilizing groups on each side. The rejuvenated Federal Trade Commission aided the formation of more effective business groups by forming and enforcing rules with whole industries, rather than individual companies, in mind. By 1979, the FTC was in severe trouble with Congress because of criticism from business groups.

A second reason for the interest groups to be concerned with Executive politics is that the Executive will shape many policies which may be amended by Congress only in their detail. Of course, interest groups often have sufficient influence in Congress to make it well worth while for the relevant Executive agency to bargain with the group in an attempt to forestall opposition. A striking, though extreme, example occurred in

1979. An unholy alliance of the normally deeply divided textile employers and unions was established to protect the industry from a reduction in tariffs on textile imports as part of the 'Tokyo Round' of multilateral trade negotiations. The coalition mustered enough strength in Congress to be able to attach an amendment prohibiting American negotiators from agreeing to a reduction in textile tariffs to a harmless bill before the Senate authorizing the Treasury to sell Carson City Silver dollars. President Carter had no choice but to veto the bill. Had the bill been passed into law, the multilateral trade negotiations would have collapsed. However, the Senators and Representatives who voted for the amendment to prohibit reductions in textile tariffs were more concerned to 'send a message' to the Office of the Special Trade Negotiator than to pass the measure into law. Indeed, most of the people voting for the textile amendment to the Carson City Silver Dollar bill probably expected a veto. However, the Special Trade Representative, the extremely experienced Texas politician Robert Strauss, recognized that if the whole trade package negotiated by him during the Tokyo Round were not to be destroyed by Congress, concessions to the textile industry were necessary. A series of talks were held between representatives of the industry and the Special Trade Representative. A compromise agreement was reached in which concessions were made by the Special Trade Representative, largely at the expense of third-world countries, sufficient to persuade the industry to endorse the package deal which Strauss had negotiated during the Tokyo Round. The textile industry's defection struck a mortal blow at the protectionist coalition which had been building in Congress, thus minimizing the difficulty of obtaining from Congress legislation to implement the Tokyo Round. Though the example of the textile industry is extreme in that no other industry was able to build such an effective coalition in its support as that industry (which had the backing of liberal Democrats linked to textile unions and conservative legislators allied to Southern employers), the example illustrates how interests with powerful support in Congress may be able to obtain concessions from an agency which realizes that it may lose even more heavily in Congress.

A further reason for the considerable attention which interests pay to the Executive is the role of the government as an ever larger consumer. The proportion of national income spent by the federal government has risen considerably in the last twenty years, and much of this money is spent on goods and services provided by outside contractors. Obtaining government custom often requires considerable lobbying. In technologically advanced industries, such as aircraft building, the links between the contractor and the Defense Department become so strong that it is in practice hard to distinguish the two. The government often provides the capital for a project, sets the technical specifications, and prescribes the production conditions. Because of the closeness of this relationship, the Defense Industry has been particularly strongly opposed to proposals to require special interests to keep a log of any contacts with officials in the Executive branch.

Techniques

It might be supposed that the lobbying methods used in dealing with the Executive branch are more technical and less obviously political than these used in lobbying Congress. After all, in spite of the enormous growth in Congressional staffs, the Executive branch has more expertise at its disposal than Congress has, or at least more technical experts. Obviously, persuasion on technical grounds does play an important part in lobbying the Executive. A close and trusting relationship is at least as important in lobbying a civil servant as in lobbying a Congressman. Until recently, however, most interest groups in the United States were too highly political, or even ideological, to provide technical information and advice as important to the Executive as their counterparts do in countries, such as Britain, with strong executives and weak legislatures. (It is interesting to compare the slow development in this respect of such well-known American interest groups as the American Farm Bureau Federation or the Chamber of Commerce with their counterparts, the National Farmers' Union and Confederation of British Industries in Great Britain.) However, any conclusion that the lobbying of the Executive branch is less 'political' than the lobbying of Congress should be rejected.

The Watergate enquiry produced many examples of leading corporations making illegal contributions to the Committee to Re-Elect the President between 1970 and 1972. It was also established that a dubious campaign contribution from milk producers was sufficient to prompt President Nixon to overrule his own Secretary of Agriculture and increase the price of milk. President Nixon's rejoinder that he was merely bidding for the farm vote and not particularly for contributions to his political slush fund is neither convincing nor edifying but serves to remind us that many Presidents, including Eisenhower and Johnson as well as Nixon, have disregarded advice from the Department of Agriculture and raised farm subsidies in election years. The textile industry, whose workers are thought to be both highly concentrated geographically and willing to cast their votes on the basis of issues related to the industry, has made every postwar Presidential candidate solicitous for the industry's welfare, no matter how deep their commitment to free trade in principle. As politicians in Britain also know, geographically concentrated blocks of voters such as farmers, textile workers, or car workers can take on a strategic importance in elections in excess of their numbers. Traditionally, however, political scientists have seen the Presidency not as the servant of special interests, but as one of the major constraints upon them.

Until recently, the dominant model of the relationship between interest groups and the Executive branch has been clientelism. Clientelism suggests that a coincidence of interests binds together interest groups, Congressional committees in the area, and the relative government department. In order to get re-elected, legislators seek committee assignments where they can serve their constituents and please the interest groups to which their voters belong; the relevant Department has to please the legislators in order to obtain legislation and appropriations which it needs; *ergo* the Congressional committees, and therefore the Department, are subservient to the relevant interest group. Even the Department Secretary must worry more about keeping the goodwill of his clients than about the policy of the President.

Whether the clientelist explanation of links between the Executive and interest groups was ever entirely true is debatable.[22] It is certainly the case that some of the Secretaries of Departments clientele theory would have predicted to have been particularly loyal to their Department's clients and disloyal to the President turned out to be entirely the opposite, namely loyal to the President and disliked by their clients. Thus relations between Secretaries of Agriculture and farmers have often been stormy, while the Secretaries' relations with the White House have been good. The clientele theory seemed to suggest that both interest groups and the relevant Congressional committees would be united in their defence of some obvious interest of their clients; in fact, many of the supposedly clientelist Departments, such as Agriculture and Labor, have been confronted with sharply divided interest groups and Congressional committees which disagree sharply about what constitutes the interests of their members. (The clientele theory must strike a Secretary of Agriculture faced with the disputes between the AFBF and NFU, the Republicans and Democrats on the House Agriculture Committee, as a simple, remote, and almost ideal situation.) Even in the case of Departments where clientele theory should work best, it often seems inaccurate.

Moreover, there seems to be a growing consensus that departments are being confronted with demands from a wider variety of interest groups. Agriculture, which once had to worry only about the difficult task of deciding between the opinions of the warring farmers' interest groups, now has to respond to pressures from ecologists and consumer groups too.[23] The Labor Department, which once was reputed to worry only about the views of the unions, now has to respond to pressure from spokesmen for women and racial minorities. It is one of the demonstrable errors of clientelism to suppose that the heads of the relevant Departments were chosen invariably from the ranks of their Department's customers, or were chosen by the relevant interest group. Few Secretaries of Labor, for example, were chosen or nominated by labour unions in the period since the Second World War.[24] However, Heclo[25] and Polsby[26] have been much struck by the very conspicuous lack of clientelistic links between President Carter's cabinet Secretaries and their Department's traditional friends. Practically none of the Carter Cabinet could be said to represent the old-line economic groups such as business, finance and labour; the Commerce Secretary, for example, Juanita Kreps, was not, as clientelism would predict, from business but was in fact an academic at Duke University. In short, though there remains disagreement about the strength of clientelism in the recent past, there is some agreement on its relative unimportance in the present.

The demise of clientele theory leaves something of a gap in the state of our knowledge about the relationship between interests and the Executive. Few contest the idea that the Executive branch in the United States is a rambling, imperfectly controlled creature. Indeed, Heclo suggests that 'issue networks', or communities of officials, outside experts, and political appointees have developed. These communities are composed of people who are interchangeable, sometimes in government, sometimes in academic establishments, and sometimes in other organizations, but always sharing similar values. Bureaucracies the world over have a tendency to assert the value of their own work and programmes over the priorities of their supposed political masters. Undoubtedly parts of the bureaucracy retain close links with interest groups outside it. Unfortunately, the situation remains confused and less determinist than clientele theory used to claim. It certainly seems that the close links between interest groups, granted a monopolistic right to speak for sectors of society and Executive Departments, are weaker, rather than stronger, in the United States than in many European countries such as Britain.

Traditionally, interest groups in the United States are thought to be more powerful than in most other countries. However, it is hard to sustain such a view of the links between interest groups and the Executive in the USA. Bureaucracies are usually said to receive two obvious benefits from dealing with interest groups. First, interest groups provide detailed information and advice beyond what the bureaucracy has at its own disposal. Second, a bureaucracy wants interest groups to supply 'consents' to policies, a guarantee that the group in question can live with a policy. American interest groups are poorly equipped to supply either information or consents. Most of the interest groups we have examined, such as the Chamber of Commerce, the Farm Bureau Federation, and the National Association of Manufacturers, have been intensely political, specializing more in arguments from first principles than in arguments based on detailed information. Not surprisingly, they have had little of a technical nature to tell bureaucrats that they did not know already. Moreover, because economic interests—labour, agriculture, and business—have been divided into competing and conflicting groups, the bureaucracies of the federal government have been unlikely to obtain a clear consent either. Until the 1970s there have been few interest groups in the United States that enjoy the respect amongst Executive officials that the CBI or the National Farmers' Union enjoy in Britain. Until recently even such fixtures of the Washington interest group scene as the Chamber of Commerce, the Farm Bureau, and the AFL-CIO have been highly political, involving themselves in numerous wide-ranging campaigns. Of late, this had been changing. There have been major attempts to improve the technical expertise of all the major business groups recently—including the American Petroleum Institute, once regarded as a highly successful lobby, but which fell on more difficult times in the early 1970s. A report by the *New York Times*[27] on the changes at the API brings out the character of these changes. The API replaced its President, a man who spent his time lobbying on Capitol Hill, by a highly educated man of whom it said his favourite work was 'analysis'. The new President, a Mr DiBona, has recruited graduate students from the best universities because he 'wanted to analyze public policy issues and to speak constructively on these issues and to seek a consensus within the industry'. In short, the API—like many business groups—realized that to date it has not excelled in those skills that do much to influence bureaucracies, and has set about changing the situation.

Conclusions

The changes in the structure of the system of interest groups in the United States has been accompanied by changes in the techniques they employ to influence politics. In some ways American interest groups are being pulled in two directions. On the one hand, the interest-group system is becoming more participatory, and more of a rough and tumble. Twenty years ago, most Washington Lobbyists sought to make friendships in a mild, restrained fashion. The labour unions were one of the comparatively few groups (along with the National Rifle Association and the American Medical Association) which regularly and systematically sought to influence the outcome of elections. The lobbyists described by Bauer, Pool, and Dexter lived in an altogether cosier world, talking to, and working with, politicians who were already their friends. Today practically every interest group has created a political action committee to channel campaign donations to its friends. Similarly, politics in the Executive branch have become more avowedly pluralist. The Departments which once were associated with but one set of interest groups (for example Agriculture with the farmers, Labor with the unions) now have conflicting claims on their attention. It is, moreover, widely agreed that the Secretaries of Departments such as Labor and Agriculture have lost influence; even within their own policy areas the Secretaries compete— not always successfully—for influence with the White House staff. Once more we return to a theme running throughout this book: the degree of overt conflict between interest groups has increased, and the veiled, cosy ties between often inefficient lobbyists and politicians' researchers found to be prevalent in the 1950s are no longer enough.

The more vigorous activity of interest groups demonstrates their adaptation to changes in the political system. At the start of this chapter we listed several factors which inhibited the power of interest groups, particularly in electoral politics, and which made it wise for lobbyists to adopt a restrained approach. Chief amongst these were the electorate's ignorance of issues and attachment to party labels, the power structure in Congress which gave the most power to the least electorally vulnerable, and procedures such as voice votes or closed committee meetings which screened legislators from public scrutiny. Most of these defences against pressure-group power have been weakened or have disappeared. Thus recent studies show that issue voting and ticket splitting have become much more important, and party identification has declined in influencing the electorate's votes.[28] Power in Congress has been widely diffused, and such pillars of the old system as seniority have crumbled. 'Sunshine' laws have opened committee hearings to the gaze of the public, or more frequently in practice to lobbyists, by making closed meetings much rarer. Recorded—roll call—votes have increased considerably in both absolute and relative terms. Moreover, campaign-finance reform, by choking off the huge contributions from a small number of 'fat cats', has made candidates more dependent on contributions from political action committees. Finally, the disappearance in many parts of the United States of parties as campaigning organizations and the increase in the number of primaries have made the electoral action organizations of interest groups even more attractive to candidates. In short, the political system has changed in ways which give interest groups more opportunity to exert pressure, and they are starting to exploit their chances.

Yet it would not be correct to suppose that interest groups have been transformed into mere small-scale variants of political parties. Indeed, in spite of the pressure for groups to be more overtly involved in electoral politics, interest groups have also to operate in a world in which policy analysis is becoming both more frequent and more developed. Even Congress, so long criticized for failing to adapt to the complexities of contemporary policy making, now has its own vast, and probably competing, bureaucracies for evaluating proposals. The old General Accounting Office and Congressional Research Service (formerly Library of Congress) have been joined in the 1970s by the Congressional Office of the Budget, the Office of Technology Evaluation, and conspicuously swollen staffs for Committees and individual legislators. All interest groups—even those with a reputation for highly ideological approaches, such as the Chamber of Commerce—felt the need to adapt. Interest groups are becoming more technical in their submissions to Congress and, even more pronouncedly, in their dealings with the Executive.

There is clearly a tension between being simultaneously more overtly involved in electoral politics and developing a reputation for technical expertise. Some groups, such as the Business Roundtable, will eschew involvement in electoral politics and rely on the prestige and expertise which large corporations possess. Yet the example of the AFL-CIO shows that it is possible to combine both approaches. By maintaining some distance between its lobbyists and its electoral action activities, the AFL-CIO has been able to employ both approaches for some time. This may be the model for the future.

The New Politics of Interests in the USA:
Towards Pluralism?

Twenty years ago it was regarded as more or less axiomatic that the American political system was pluralist, and that this was one of its desirable features.[1] The highly visible and supposedly important role played by interest groups was an important piece of evidence supporting this belief. Two elements were particularly important in the pluralist picture of American politics. The first—really a conclusion—was that power was widely dispersed amongst numerous interests and that every group enjoyed significant opportunities to influence policy. The second element in the pluralist account of American politics was the conception of the nature of power. The power of groups could be assessed by a comparison of their resources, or by observing who won, and who lost, when interests collided in the political arena. Pluralists contended that the exercise of political power was observable and hence its distribution measurable. There were no hidden sources of power, or power élites which modified the distribution of power between the numerous competing groups visible to all.

Pluralism, never universally accepted as a prescriptive theory and occasionally challenged empirically, was one of the casualties of the 1960s. Numerous objections to the theory were raised. Schattschneider observed that many groups were not represented effectively within the pressure-group system. The poor, in particular, were not represented adequately so that 'the pluralist choir sang with an upper class accent.'[2] General and important interests which affected everyone to some degree were neglected precisely because no minority was affected heavily: following Olson,[3] political scientists observed that a rational political actor would not join a pressure group which pressed for more effective air-pollution controls because everyone would benefit, while only people joining the group would bear the costs. Only if individualized benefits were made available would rational political actors organize to protect public goods such as clean air.

More fundamental questions about the accuracy of pluralist analyses of the power of interests were raised by Bachrach and Baratz.[4] Pluralist analysis concentrated on observable clashes between interests such as conflicts between labour and management over labour-relations laws. Pluralists did not recognize the importance of a particularly important kind of power, the power to control the agenda and prevent discussion of issues at all. Lukes went even further and, applying the Marxist concept of false consciousness, argued that certain sectors of society had the power to control how, if at all, people perceived their interests and so could prevent any conceptualization of a challenge to their own interests.[5] Finally, Lindblom, previously associated with the pluralist tradition, pointed to the structural factors in market economies which gave business a stronger, privileged position over other interest groups in society. Because businessmen were entrusted with the essential social tasks of generating and distributing wealth, politicians must deal with them not as mere pressure-group officials but as equals. We may recall Lindblom's concise statement of the agreement:

Any government official who understands the requirements of his position and the responsibilities that market orientated systems throw on businessmen will therefore grant them a privileged position. Nor does he have to be an uncritical admirer of businessmen to do so. He does not have to be bribed, duped or pressured to do so. He simply understands as is plain to see that public affairs in market orientated society are in the hands of two groups of leaders, government and business and that to make the system work, government leadership must often defer to business leadership.[6]

If business demands are rejected and business confidence lost, investment and prosperity will suffer. Business has a power which owes nothing to votes or orthodox political campaigning. The criticisms of pluralism by Bachrach and Baratz, Lukes and Lindblom, contained a common theme. The distribution of power in society was not, as pluralists supposed, directly observable. No amount of attention to the manoeuvrings of interest groups or other political actors would yield an accurate picture of why some benefited and others lost from public policy. In particular, business groups benefited from the 'second' and 'third' faces of power which pluralist analysis could not unmask.

Although the debates between pluralists and their critics were fierce, few challenged the proposition that if interest groups are important anywhere, it is in the United States. In spite of a dearth of comparative studies, it remained the accepted wisdom that interest groups were unusually powerful in the USA. In fact, however, nearly all the obvious economic interests were much less well organized and represented politically in the United States than in most western democracies.

By the mid 1970s it was quite possible to assert that many European states were 'neo-corporatist'.[7] Though the precise meaning of this somewhat derogatory label has never been entirely clear, it is possible to provide a rough summary of what a neo-corporatist political system looks like. Important policy decisions are made by governments only after extensive consultation, approximating negotiations, with economic interest groups such as unions and employers' organizations given a monopolistic right to represent their sector of society, and sometimes to make binding commitments on behalf of their members to the government. Such agreements typically involved some modification of the behaviour in which groups would otherwise have engaged. For example, unions might accept wage restraint, employers lower price increases or guidance in their investment plans, and governments some change in their social or tax policies after tripartite or neo-corporatist discussions. In short, economic interest groups in many European states became important (though perhaps not equal) partners with government in the formation of policy.

There is little doubt that this pattern of close partnership between interest groups and government never became established in the United States. Why the United States never become neo-corporatist is a subject which can be, and has been, discussed at some length.[8] Explanations can be framed in terms of both the structure of government and political culture of the United States. 'The government' of the United States is not a relatively cohesive and easily defined group of people as in the Parliamentary systems of Western Europe (and, for that matter, of the French Fifth Republic). Instead 'the government' in the

United States is divided into three branches and innumerable sub-units at the national level, and power is shared with state governments which suffer from at least as much fragmentation. In short, there is no cohesive government with which economic interests could deal authoritatively, and equally the fragmentation of government makes it impossible to limit access to decision making to a few recognized interest groups, a practice common, for example, in British government. Moreover, government, or perhaps governments in the United States have accepted, and perhaps are expected by the public to accept, fewer responsibilities than in other Western democratic regimes. In particular, economic policies which oblige governments to seek the co-operation of economic interest groups such as planning and incomes policies have found little favour in the USA; experiments with either have been short lived. In spite of a sharp increase over the last twenty years, the proportion of national income spent by government in the United States remains less than in other Western countries, and at present there is a significant backlash against high—or supposedly high—levels of taxation and possibly against the provision of greater government services.

Yet one of the major factors explaining the absence of neo-corporatism in the United States is the weakness of the interest groups themselves. In almost every respect, economic interest groups in the United States are less impressive than their European counterparts and less attractive for government to bargain with. All economic groups—employers, farmers, and unions—recruit a smaller percentage of potential members than their counterparts in northern Europe. Moreover, economic sectors are typically represented politically by not one unified body (such as the National Farmers' Union), as is the pattern in Britain, but by several conflicting groups (such as the American Farm Bureau Federation, the National Farmers' Union, the National Farmers' Organization, and the Grange). American economic interest groups, such as the Chamber of Commerce or the Farm Bureau, had a high reputation for ideological fervour and a low reputation for supplying reliable useful information. Indeed, American politicians, who are obliged by the nature of electoral politics to put more effort into discovering their constituents' opinions on issues than is common in Europe, have frequently expressed doubts about the representativeness of interest groups' leaders. Major studies of lobbyists for interest groups found that there were frequent comments made by officials and politicians doubting the technical and political competence of lobbyists.[9]

Some individual *interests* of course were very adequately represented within the political system. The oil companies had many friends within the Congress; so had military contractors. The ease with which these individual interests could achieve considerable influence over certain aspects of public policy (such as the oil-depletion allowance) was one reason why more impressive umbrella interest groups were not created; politically aware industries had no need to seek support from others. Another and more important reason for the weakness of interest groups was the weakness of the challenge from organized labour in the United States. In Europe strong unions had prompted the formation of strong employers' organizations; the emergence of both had prompted interests, such as farmers, to create pressure groups too. In the United States, in contrast, unions have organized a low proportion of the workforce (some 21 per cent at present) and a significant section of the union movement has been notably conservative and inactive politically. Employers have not been pushed into organizing to offset union power. In this sense the answer to the question why the close, neo-corporatist links between government and interests common in Europe is absent in the United States is to be found in the same area as the answer to Sombart's classic question about the absence of socialism in the United States.[10] Both questions are ultimately connected to the limited industrial development of the labour movement in the USA.

The unions were in fact, though weak industrially, well organized politically. Indeed, a recent textbook on American interest groups comments: 'In the early 1970s, organised labor, notably the AFL-CIO came closer than any other major national group to meeting the varied demands of modern lobbying.'[11] This developed political capability constituted a major break with the Gompers tradition of a-political business unionism in the United States. Though the emergence of industrial unionism in the CIO unions had prepared the ground for this change, it was precipitated by the passing of the Taft–Hartley Act which made clear to unions that even their purely industrial work could be affected most seriously by legislation; unions were in fact vulnerable to political attack and hostile legislation. The AFL-CIO went on to develop a body, the Committee on Political Education, which was one of the most efficient campaigning organizations in America, and to employ some of the most highly respected lobbyists in Washington. Yet though the AFL-CIO was able to make notable contributions to the campaigns for general liberal domestic policies on civil rights and poverty, the unions were never able to make much progress on changing labour-relations laws to their own advantage. Republicans and Southern Democrats, ideologically hostile and representing suburbs or states where unions were weak, were steady in their support for the rights of management against unions.

Less predictable, and more disconcerting for the unions, was the tendency for significant numbers of liberal Democrats, allied to the unions on many policy issues and recieving help from them in elections, to desert them on labour-law issues. In spite of considerable liberal Democratic strength in Congress in 1958–60, 1964–6, and 1974–8, unions were unable to secure even moderate changes in the labour-relations laws designed to remove loop-holes that unscrupulous employers could exploit. In the American political culture with its vestiges of the 'liberal tradition' described by Hartz, it was easy to whip up feeling against unions, while a corrupt minority of union leaders gave plausibility to attacks on unions in general. The unions' high level of political organization was thus more an attempt to compensate for political vulnerability than a sign of strength.[12]

Conversely, business interests saw little need to be conspicuously active in politics in the 1950s. Until the 1960s business basked in a favourable political culture. Social scientists described 'the end of ideology' so that fundamental questions about society were no longer raised. It was one of the numerous millionaires in President Eisenhower's Cabinet who made the (admittedly somewhat controversial) remark that what was good for General Motors was good for the United States and vice versa. Opinion polls showed that the general public had considerable respect for business leaders. The workings of the seniority system in Congress placed in the most powerful positions of that institution politicians most likely to take a sympathetic attitude to business. The atmosphere of the Cold War and McCarthyism played an important part in damping down radical social thought and criticism.

Not surprisingly, in this climate only industries particularly dependent on the government for contracts or handouts (such as the military contractors and the oil companies) were politically alert. Not only were peak associations, such as the Chamber of Commerce or the National Association of Manufacturers, conspicuously poorly organized and the trade associations for most industries regarded with genial contempt by politicians, but even major companies were politically inactive. Thus International Telephone and Telegraph had no Washington office until the early 1960s and one of the reasons why General Motors did poorly in its controversy with Ralph Nader over the safety of the Corvair was that it had no permanent representation in Washington. Nader was able to maintain better links with legislators and their aides than the giant motor company was. As we have seen, it was the considered opinion of Dita Beard, that in the early 1970s her employers were inadequately informed about how political decisions are made: ' . . . within a very short time I realised that none of them knew the name of the game in Washington. They had no political representation. They were babes in arms.' [13]

Numerous indices can be used to show that the efforts made by several economic interests to influence policy-making have increased dramatically. No interest shows a larger increase in organized political activity than business. The first stirrings of greater formal involvement in politics by business go back to the early 1960s when ex-President Eisenhower and the Chamber of Commerce launched a campaign to persuade businessmen to involve themselves in politics. The Business-Industry Political Action Committee (BIPAC) was formed as a result of this upswing in activity in 1963. Why the business community felt a greater need to involve itself in politics in the early 1960s is unclear. Although the underlying motivation may have been an awareness of the growing importance of government decisions to business in general, businessmen managed to conjure political danger, if not out of thin air, at least out of the surprising source of the Kennedy administration. The Kennedy advisors were perceived as liberal; there was a notable fight over steel prices.

The landslide victory for the Democrats which brought many liberals into Congress in the 1964 elections and permanently weakened the conservative grip on that institution provided further impetus. The increase in business's political activity during this period should not be exaggerated, and is in any case hard to measure precisely. For the form that much of the increased political involvement took was the making of illegal campaign contributions. Federal law (18 US Code 610) forbade corporations to make campaign contributions. Yet a substantial proportion—said by prosecutors to be one-third—of the Fortune 500 largest companies established secret and illegal funds for making political contributions. Typically—as with the Minnesota Mining and Manufacturing Corporation, for example—these funds made numerous relatively small contributions to politicians spanning the mainstream of the political spectrum, from liberals such as Hubert Humphrey to prominent Republicans such as Senator Scott, Republican leader in the Senate and for long a recipient of funds from Gulf Oil. Politicians regarded taking illegal, if limited, contributions from companies as part of normal politics and were surprised when the companies fearing prosecution, ended their contributions.[14]

We have seen that illegal campaign contributions, such as ITT's offer of substantial funds to help Republicans meet President Nixon's wish to hold the 1972 Convention in San Diego were made, with the hope of influencing a specific government decision. In general, however, we concluded that the payments were probably a means of securing access to decision makers for the companies.[15]

Developments in the early 1970s made it impossible for major companies to rely indefinitely on such haphazard techniques for influencing policy. One reason for changing the system was that it became apparent that illegally buying access to decision makers could be used by those decision makers to extort payments from companies. Nixon's Committee to Re-Elect the President in particular blackmailed many prominent companies such as American Airlines for campaign contributions much larger than those given illegally and voluntarily. The most obvious example of such blackmail, which was described in Chapter 4, was the way the Nixon Administration extorted illegal campaign contributions from American Airlines. As the example showed, in a sense the illegal campaign contributions from business exposed after Watergate demonstrated not the strength but the vulnerability of business. This vulnerability had been increased considerably by a most important phenomenon, the rise of the public interest groups. It is possible to offer numerous reasons for the prominence which public interest groups attained in the early 1970s. Many of the groups—particularly those concerned with protecting the environment and improving the honesty and efficiency of government—were able to draw on long-standing traditions in American politics. Indeed, several public interest groups (such as the Auduban Society) had long been in existence. Yet the public interest groups returned with much greater vigour than for fifty years, and with an approach to the public interest based more on adversary politics than on a claim to represent the only honest approach, something often alleged to be true of the public interest groups in an earlier period. Perhaps the affluence of American society encouraged people to be concerned about less immediate interests than in the recent past, to take up issues less obviously concerned with redistributive issues or class-based politics. Certainly the evidence available suggests that the public interest groups drew disproportionately upon the professional middle classes for support. Perhaps the general sceptical mood in the USA in the 1960s helped public interest groups, and a series of incidents—oil spills off California, the resistance of motor manufacturers to measures to improve safety, and the supervision of the constitution by the Committee to Re-Elect the President—demonstrated vividly that the concerns of the public interest groups were not figments of the imagination. Yet though technological changes often created problems which public interest groups complained about, some technological changes helped the public interest groups by making possible direct mailing appeals and low-cost long-distance telephone campaigns.

Explanations of the rise of the public interest groups in the late 1960s will probably remain highly speculative. It is clear, however, that by the mid 1970s the public interest groups had achieved considerable strength and seemed likely to make further progress. Membership grew rapidly. Common Cause, founded in 1970, had 325,000 members by 1974. Nader's Public

Citizen foundation claimed 175,000 contributors and the Sierra Club 153,000.[17] The comparatively affluent and educated people who constitute this membership are a valuable political resource. They are people from social groups most willing and able to participate in politics by writing to legislators, following votes in Congress in the media, and firing off telegrams and letters in time to influence them. Lobbyists for public interest groups, speaking for such apparently admirable causes as a cleaner and safer environment or honesty in government, were treated with a degree of respect not accorded to other lobbyists. Both politicians and the press were unusually receptive to the public interest groups, and lobbyists for such groups were able to generate enough pressure by the active membership or by events easy for the media to portray (such as announcing awards to the Dirty Dozen legislators with the worst voting record on environmental issues) to keep both politicians and media impressed.

The period from 1968 to 1976 was a period of great success for the public interest groups. Stricter legislation on consumer and environmental protection were obtained, and the system of campaign finance recast. The Federal Trade Commission was revivified and began to apply its regulations more vigorously. New agencies of great enthusiasm and determination were created. Of particular importance were the Federal Elections Commission, the Environmental Protection Agency, and the Occupational Safety and Health Administration, the latter of course also receiving considerable backing from the unions.

The rise of the public interest groups had important consequences for both our argument and other groups. The success of the public interest groups most obviously meant that issues and interests which had not received much attention in the past, and which political scientists following Olson had believed could not be organized were now well represented. Even that tiny fish, the snail darter, found articulate friends; a dam which would have destroyed its habitat was blocked under the Endangered Species Act. There were powerful voices for clean air, more honest advertising, more honest government, and the numerous other general but important interests which writers in the 1950s had rightly reported to be unrepresented. (This is not to argue that the success of the public interest groups necessarily refutes Olson; indeed many, as he would have advised, reinforced their member's commitment to public goods with benefits available only to members.) This development was itself of great importance to the structure of American interest-group politics. The second major consequence of the rise of public interest groups was the effect on other groups. In particular, the successes of public interest groups usually seemed to be at the expense of business, or at least of short-term business interests. The impact of environmental legislation and the EPA affected such a variety of industries—from oil companies in Alaska to (through their smokestacks) steel companies in Pittsburgh that it was much more the case that general business interests were (at least in the minds of businessmen) at risk.

Indeed it could be argued plausibly that much the legislation of which businessmen complained had been passed in part because of the failure of the business community to protect its collective interests adequately. It was precisely an issue such as pollution that affected all industries rather than a few firms (as military contracts would) that was likely to expose the weakness in business's representation in Washington. It is a sign of how poorly articulated perfectly reasonable business interests were that Congress passed, by huge majorities or sometimes almost unanimously, measures which contained unreasonable requirements or instructions to regulatory agencies. The instruction to the EPA, for example, to end pollution without regard to cost, thus paved the way for complaints of over-regulation. Advocacy of better protection for consumers, and even the exposure by Common Cause of illegal corporate campaign contributions, seemed to businessmen to show that their collective interests were under attack. The decline of the Republican Party and the influx of liberal Democrats after Watergate (who shifted Congressional procedures in their favour too) convinced many businessmen that their interests were vulnerable to further attack. In contrast, public interest groups, allied with agencies they had helped create (such as the EPA) seemed likely to go from strength to strength.

The years since 1974 have seen a remarkable increase in all overt forms of business involvement in politics. Taking advantage of a fortuitous change in campaign-finance laws, ironically introduced in 1972 primarily to protect the political action committees of labour unions, companies have become major sources of campaign funds. Under current campaign-finance legislation companies can meet the costs of creating and running political action committees which disburse funds collected from managers, shareholders, and, on two occasions a year, employees. In 1974 there were eighty-nine political action committees created by companies; in 1978 there were 776 supplying funds equivalent to 15 per cent of total campaign contributions. [18] Nor do the new business action committees give money only to conservative politicians. On the contrary, and sensibly, companies give their money to those most likely to win—incumbents—and those with the most influence, such as committee chairmen. Over half the money from company PACs goes to Democrats, and the bulk of this money goes to liberal Democrats also supported by liberal groups such as the more political unions. (Senator Kennedy has been an example of a recipient of funds in his Senate campaigns from business on both these grounds.) PACs met 60 per cent of the House expenses of House committee chairmen and 20 per cent of the expense of Senate committee chairmen. [19] Though PACs are limited by the 1974 Campaign Finance Act to donations of $5,000 per primary and per election, it is somewhat amusing to note that several powerful legislators have received campaign contributions in excess of their expenditures. To the irritation of their conservative friends, businessmen have given money to politicians with the most power, and at present in Congress many of these politicians are, by American standards, liberal.

There has been a corresponding increase in the level of lobbying by business. Individual companies have increased their representation in Washington considerably. ITT, for example, which in the early 1960s was scarcely represented in Washington, was able by the early 1970s to mount one of the most vigorous of recent lobbying campaigns in an attempt to block the anti-trust action brought by the Justice Department. Subsequent investigations were to show that ITT had launched what one of its internal memoranda called a campaign of 'inexorable pressure' in which its President had seventeen meetings with Cabinet level officials (including the President's top aides, Haldeman and Ehrlichman). ITT's ability to launch a sustained lobbying campaign reflected the growth of lobbying on the part of many companies. Epstein has shown that whereas Bauer, Pool, and Dexter found that the vast majority of firms did not lobby at all, Epstein found that just over half the large firms he surveyed monitored legislation continuously.[20] From 1974 to 1978 the number of lobbyists for corporations in Washington increased from 8,000 to 15,000, and this growth continues. Of greater significance have been the attempts to equip business with effective umbrella organizations defending the general concerns of business. The Business Roundtable, to which 180 of the *Fortune* 500 now belong was formed as an entirely new organization, to represent the collective interests of large companies. In contrast to the reputation of older business umbrella groups, the Roundtable has sought to create an image of technical expertise and pragmatism rather than repeating automatically conservative slogans. The commissioning of high-quality research and the use of top company executives to lobby legislators has helped to create the desired impression. Indeed, Shapiro became a close confidant of President Carter and the Roundtable won considerable prestige in Congress after it arranged a deal between business and pro-Israel groups on how to legislate on Arab sanctions on companies dealing with Israel.

The older business umbrella groups faced with this competition have themselves tried to improve their image and their effectiveness. In particular, the Chamber of Commerce has achieved a substantial improvement in its membership and status. Between 1967 and 1976, membership of the Chamber rose from 35,686 to 61,578.[21] Instead of doctrinaire conservatism, the Chamber has adopted a more reasoned approach. On some issues the Chamber has supported policies also favoured by liberals (such as the provision of day-care facilities for children of working parents, or the creation of public-service jobs to counteract the recession of 1973–6.) On other issues the Chamber has attempted to provide more reasoned arguments for conservative views than in the past rather than retreating immediately to basic principles such as arguments that the issue is not a federal responsibility. The performance of the Chamber's lobbyists has improved considerably. Indeed, the Chamber has not only taken over some of the techniques pioneered by unions and public interest groups but raised them to new heights of efficiency. Somewhat ironically, the Chamber has made itself the acknowledged expert on participatory lobbying. It has refined the efficiency of its organization to the point where within a week it can carry out research on the impact of a bill on each legislator's district and through its local branches mobilize a 'grass-roots campaign' on the issue in time to affect the outcome of the vote. On issues which mature more slowly, such as reform of the labour-relations laws in 1978, the Chamber has shown that it can now do better than unions or public interest groups in bringing large numbers of people to Washington or mobilizing them to buttonhole their legislator when he or she is home for the weekend. The Chamber, in short, is no longer a laughing-stock amongst Washington lobbyists; indeed, it is now a pace-setter.[22]

The last few years have seen business benefit from this upsurge in their lobbying and other forms of political action. Labour unions suffered defeats in Congress on their attempts to legalize common situs picketing in the construction industry and to reform the labour-relations laws so as to make it difficult for employers to refuse to deal with unions supported by their employees. On both occasions business groups launched vigorous lobbying campaigns which surprised legislators and, on the first occasion, unions, with their thoroughness. Public interest groups, supported by the unions, were dealt a blow when Congress refused to create a Consumer Advocacy Agency to appear before bodies such as regulatory commissions to argue on behalf of consumers. Thus the period in which reform could be slipped past unsuspecting business groups had certainly been brought to an end. Business had turned the tide, moreover, in unpromising political circumstances. After the 1974 elections the number of supposedly liberal Democrats in Congress rose sharply, and did not fall significantly. The conjuncture of a heavily Democratic Congress and the election in 1976 of a Democratic President seemed to provide the best opportunity since 1964 for a flood of legislation of a type most unwelcome to business. Though in 1978 the 'taxpayers' revolt' made the achievement of major reforms unlikely, business had already defeated most of the proposed reforms it disliked most intensely. Nor was this surprising. Business groups had become sophisticated lobbyists and bigger campaign contributors than unions.

Indeed, if the combined total of business groups and their allies, such as the American Medical Association or Realtors, are taken into account, business gave more than unions by a margin of two to one. Business had learnt how to play pluralist politics.

The balance between economic groups in politics has therefore, in a sense, been restored. Business, which in the 1950s went almost unchallenged, is now back in a secure political position. The public interest groups which shocked business into action have seen their fortunes decline. Public interest groups have suffered legislative reverses; they have also seen membership fall (though not back to pre-1970 levels) and greater scepticism amongst both commentators and politicians about them developed. It is more common to find even writers of academic studies quoting with approval the comment of a business lobbyist that Common Cause is but one interest and viewpoint amongst many. Indeed, several politicians have complained that public interest groups are as capable of sharp practice (such as rigging Congressional voting scores) as any other group. Indeed, the odd voice has been heard suggesting that there is a conspicuous lack of democracy in Nader's public interest groups. Meanwhile unions seem to continue their inexorable industrial decline, unable, in spite of their political action, to build enough support to make the change in labour-relations laws so essential if this decline is to be arrested.

Yet if the balance between economic groups has been restored, it has been recreated out of new resources. No longer does business win without trying, as it once did. Business now wins its battles by using the standard interest-group techniques such as lobbying and campaign contributions. In a sense economic interests have been 'politicized' or at least drawn into politics to a degree unusual in the United States. What the consequences will be for economic interests is unclear. No doubt factors other than interst-group tactics such as ideology and the need to preserve business confidence continue to give business a more privileged position than that enjoyed by other interests. However, the change in the political basis of the balance between economic groups does have obvious implications for the political system. The degree to which politicians in the USA are acting under pressure and scrutiny has increased. The activities of the non-economic groups, particularly the new single issue groups, are certainly important. Yet in terms of the number of lobbyists and the size of campaign contributions, it is the politicized economic interests that make the greatest impact. Interest groups have come to play a more obvious and important role in American politics in the last ten years. Whether this makes the creation of public policy on contentious issues any easier is to be doubted.

The theoretical implications of these changes are also interesting. In the days when everyone accepted that the United States was a pluralist political system in which interest groups played a major role, such groups were in fact very weak. Apart from the fact that many of the public interest groups did not exist or were unnoticed, even powerful interests in society did not feel that it was necessary to be organized politically to defend collective interests. Groups often cited in textbooks as powerful and impressive organizations turned out, on closer inspection, to have conspicuous weaknesses in terms of membership, organization, and standing in Washington. Though the Farm Bureau, the Chamber of Commerce, and the National Association of Manufacturers usually merited a mention in the 'interest groups' chapter of books on American politics, there was no evidence to suggest that these groups exerted a major influence on policy. Groups such as business often gained the most from policy in spite of the fact that their observable power resources, the power resources such as interest-group activity which pluralists had emphasized, were unimpressive. Now groups are well organized, and it is at least the conventional wisdom around Washington that the new generation of lobbyists and political action committees exert significant pressure on politicians and are better equipped as suppliers of advice and information. Interest groups have come closer, in short, to playing the role they always were supposed to—but did not—in American politics.

Of course, this does not destroy the validity of some of the criticisms made of pluralism. Some issues, particularly those to do with poverty, disadvantage, and redistribution are hard to place on the agenda for discussion. The wave of enthusiasm for tax-cutting, abolishing regulation of many industries, and generally limiting the growth of government reminds us that the liberal tradition of the American ideology is not dead. In the period since the collapse of the Bretton Woods international monetary system, which sheltered American economic policy from international pressures, the economic contraints on American policy makers have tightened to an important degree. American Administrations, like British governments, can now be forced into 'U' turns by speculation against their currency overseas, something which was impossible when all currencies were 'pegged' to the dollar. Yet the fact remains that interests which once played little part in politics now feel the need to do so. This change is surely of significance. At least the reasons why some interests win and others lose are now a little more open and observable, and in that sense, pluralist.

Notes

Chapter 1

[1] Alexis de Tocqueville, *Democracy in America*, Vol. i, chapter XII, Vol. ii, chapter 5, Alfred Knopf, New York, 1966.

[2] William Kornhauser, *The Politics of Mass Society*, Routledge & Kegan Paul, London, 1960, p. 74.

[3] As we shall see, these descriptions of economic interests by public interest groups such as Common Cause and leaders such as Ralph Nader are common.

[4] Harold Dwight Lasswell, *Who Gets What, When, How*, Mc Graw-Hill, New York, 1936.

[5] Tocqueville, op. cit.

[6] In Alexander Hamilton, James Madison, John Jay, *The Federalist Papers*, (ed. Clinton Rossiter), Mentor Books, No. 10, New York, 1961.

[7] David Truman, *The Governmental Process*, Alfred Knopf, New York, 1951.

[8] For a useful discussion see John Gray, 'On the Contestability of Social and Political Concepts', *Political Theory*, 5 (1977), 331–48.

[9] Robert Dahl, *Who Governs?*, Yale University Press, New Haven, 1961.

[10] E. E. Schattschneider, *The Semi-Sovereign People*, Holt Reinhart, Winston, New York, 1960.

[11] Peter Bachrach and Morton Baratz, 'The Two Faces of Power', *APSR* 1962, and *Power and Poverty: Theory and Practice*, Oxford University Press, London and Toronto, 1970.

[12] Matthew Crenson, *The Un-Politics of Air Pollution, A Study of Non Decisionmaking in the Cities*, Johns Hopkins Press, Baltimore, 1971, pp. 42, 68.

[13] Steven Lukes, *Power, A Radical View*, Macmillan, London, 1974.

[14] Brian Barry, 'The Obscurities of Power', *Government and Opposition* (10), 1975.

[15] Charles E. Lindblom, *Politics and Markets, The World's Political-Economic Systems*, Basic Books, New York, 1977.

[16] Lindblom, op. cit.

[17] Ibid.

Chapter 2

[1] US Senate, Committee on Agriculture and Forestry, 89th Congress 1st Session, *Farm Programs and Dynamic Forces in Agriculture*, tables 4 and 5; Luther G. Tweeten, Earl O. Meady, and Les U. Mayer, *Farm Program Alternatives*, CAED Report 18, Iowa State University 1963; Charles Schultz, *The Distribution of Farm Subsidies. Who Gets the Benefits?*, Brookings Institution Staff Paper, Washington DC, 1971.

[2] R. G. Lipsey, *An Introduction to Positive Economics*, Weidenfeld & Nicholson, London, 1974.

[3] Andrew Shonfield, *Modern Capitalism, The Changing Balance of Public and Private Power*, Oxford University Press, Oxford, 1965.

[4] Christina McFadyen Campbell, *The Farm Bureau and the New Deal*, University of Illinois Press, Urbana, 1962, p. 92.

[5] Wesley McCune, *Who's Behind our Farm Policy?*, Praeger, New York, 1956, p. 15.

[6] O. M. Kile, *The Farm Bureau through Three Decades*, Waverly Press, Baltimore, 1948, p. 60.

[7] Kile, op. cit., p. 62.

[8] See Samuel Berger, *Dollar Harvest*, Heath Lexington, Lexington (Mass.), 1971.

[9] Mancur Olson, *The Logic of Collective Action*, Shocken Books, New York, 1969.

[10] See Berger, op. cit.

[11] The examples of Farm Bureau policies are taken from their annual leaflet, *Farm Bureau Policies*.

[12] D. E. Morrison and W. Keith Warner, 'Correlates of Farmers' Attitudes towards Public and Private Aspects of Agricultural Organisation', *Rural Sociology*, 1971.

[13] US Congress, House of Representatives, Committee on Agriculture 86th Congress 1st Session, *General Farm Legislation*, 1959, p. 256.

[14] US Congress, Committee on Agriculture, Hearings, *General Farm and Food Stamp Program*, Serial Q, 1969.

[15] US Congress, House of Representatives, Committee on Agriculture, Subcommittee on Livestock and Grains, *General Farm and Food Stamp Program*, p. 1121.

[16] Proceedings of the 1968 Convention, official minutes.

[17] US Congress, Committee on Agriculture, 86th Congress, 1st Session, Hearings, *General Farm Legislation*, 1959, p. 145.

[18] John Kenneth Galbraith, *American Capitalism, The Concept of Countervailing Power*, Hamish Hamilton, London, 1957.

[19] National Farmers' Union, policy statement, 1972.

[20] A. J. Crampton, *The National Farmers' Union, Ideology of a Pressure Group*, University of Nebraska Press, Lincoln, Nebraska, 1965, p. 59.

[21] E. Shils, *The Torment of Secrecy*, The Free Press, Glencoe, 1956 p. 99; Seymour Martin Lipset, *Political Man*, Heineman Educational Books, London, 1969.

[22] Michael Paul Rogin, *The Intellectuals and McCarthy. The Radical Spectre*, MIT Press, Cambridge (Mass.), 1967.

Chapter 3

[1] J. David Greenstone, *Unions in American Politics*, Alfred Knopf, New York, 1969.

[2] Louis Reed, *The Labor Philosophy of Samuel Gompers*, Kennikat Press, New York, 1966, pp. 106, 117.

[3] Steven Brill, *The Teamsters*, Simon & Schuster, New York, 1978, esp. pp. 100–6.

[4] Matthew Josephson, *Sidney Hillman, Statesman of Labor*, Doubleday & Co., New York, 1952, p. 662.

[5] Philip Taft, *Labor Politics American Style*, The California State Federation of Labor, Harvard University Press, Cambridge (Mass.), 1969.

[6] Frank W. McCulloch and Tim Bernstein, *The National Labor Relations Board*, Praeger, New York, 1974.

[7] *Congressional Quarterly Weekly Report*, 'The AFL-CIO: How Much Clout in Congress.' (19 July 1975), pp. 1531–40.

[8] *Washington Post*, 13 Apr. 1972.

[9] *Congressional Quarterly Weekly Report*, 1975, op. cit.

[10] Ibid.

[11] For further discussion of the role of unions in elections, see Graham K. Wilson, *Unions in American National Politics*, Macmillan, London, 1979.

[12] Irving Richter, *Political Purpose in Trade Unions*, George Allen & Unwin, London, 1973, esp. pp. 196–7.

[13] Angus Campbell, Philip Converse, Warren Miller, and Donald Stokes, *The American Voter*, John Wiley, New York and London, 1964; Norman Nie, Sidney Verba, J. R. Petrocik, *The Changing American Voter*, Harvard University Press, Cambridge (Mass.), 1976.

[14] Arthur Kornhauser, Harold Sheppard, Albert Mayer, *When Labor Votes*, A Study of Auto Workers, New York, University Books, 1956. For more recent data see Harold L. Sheppard and Nicholas A. Masters, 'The Political Attitudes and Preferences of Union Members; the Case of the Detroit Auto Workers', *APSR* 1959 and Norman Blume, 'The Impact of a Labor Union on its Membership in a Local Election', *Western Political Quarterly*, XXIII. (March 1970).

[15] Sheppard and Masters, op. cit.

[16] See Wilson, op. cit., p. 22.

[17] Speech by Walter Reuther to the Wharten School of Finance and Commerce, 25 Nov. 1966 (UAW transcript).

Chapter 4

[1] Karl Marx, Friedrich Engels, *The Communist Manifesto*, part 1. 'The executive committee of the modern state is but a committee for managing the common affairs of the whole bourgeoisie.'

[2] Charles E. Lindblom, *Politics and Markets*, Basic Books, New York, 1977.

[3] Ibid., p. 175 (emphasis added).

[4] Ibid., P. 185.

[5] Charles Dickens, *Hard Times*, 1898 ed., pp. 123–4.

[6] US Congress, Senate, 92nd Congress 2nd Session, Committee on the Judiciary, *Nomination of Richard G. Kleindienst to Serve as Attorney General* (hereafter *Kleindienst hearings*), p. 745.

[7] Raymond Bauer, Ithiel de Sola Pool, and Anthony Lewis Dexter, *American Business and Public Policy*. Prentice Hall International, London and New York, 1964.

[8] Ibid., p. 111.

[9] Ibid., p. 324.

[10] Ibid., p. 353.

[11] Adam Yarmolinsky, *The Military Establishment*, Harper & Row, New York, Evanston, London, 1977.

[12] See Robert Engler, *The Brotherhood of Oil*, University of Chicago Press, Chicago and London, 1977.

[13] C. Wright Mills, *The Power Élite*, Oxford University Press, London and New York, 1956.

[14] G. William Domhoff, *Who Rules America?*, Prentice Hall International, Englewood Cliffs, N.J., 1967.

[15] Richard Gable, 'NAM: Influential Lobby or Kiss of Death?' *Journal of Politics*, 1953.

[16] 'The Chamber and the NAM—A Marriage of Convenience', *National Journal*, 7 Aug. 1976.

[17] 'US Chamber Works to Erase Negative Image and Improve Grass Roots Clout', *National Journal*, 1 Apr. 1972.

[18] 'The Chamber and the NAM—Marriage of Convenience', *National Journal*, 7 Aug. 1976.

[19] *New York Times*, 11 Feb. 1962.

[20] *New York Times*, 10 Oct. 1962.

[21] For a discussion of these factors see Jim F. Heath, *John F. Kennedy and the Business Community*, University of Chicago Press, Chicago and London, 1969.

[22] *Kleindienst hearings*, p. 770 (emphasis added).

[23] *New York Times*, 7 June 1962.

[24] *New York Times*, 1 July 1962.

[25] *New York Times*, 5 Aug. 1963.

[26] US Senate, Select Committee on Presidential Campaign Activities (hereafter 'Ervin Committee') 93rd Congress, 1st Session *Watergate and Related Matters*, Phase III, *Campaign Financing*, p. 5405.

[27] *New York Times*, 13 Jan. 1976; Louis M. Kohlmeier, 'Beyond the Tip of the Iceberg', *National Journal*, 10 Jan. 1976.

[28] *New York Times*, 17 Apr. 1975.

[29] *New York Times*, 12 Mar. 1975.

[30] *New York Times*, 1 Jan. 1975.

[31] *New York Times*, 4 Jan. 1976.

[32] US Senate Ervin Committee Hearngs, Phase III, *Campaign Financing*, p. 5447.

[33] Edward M. Epstein, *The Corporation in American Politics*, Prentice Hall International, Englewood Cliffs, N.J., 1969.

[34] See *Kleindienst hearings*, p. 98; and in particular, Executive Report, pp. 92–19, Part 4, Mr Kennedy from the Judiciary Committee, Individual Views: Anthony Sampson, *Sovereign State; Secret History of International Telephone and Telegraph*, Hodder, London, 1973.

[35] For the text of the memo, see *Kleindienst hearings*.

[36] US Congress, House of Representatives, Calendar No. 426, *Impeachment of Richard M. Nixon, President of the United States*, Report from the Committee on the Judiciary.

[37] US Congress, House of Representatives, Committee on the Judiciary, *Impeachment of Richard M. Nixon, President of the United States*, Book V, Part 1, Department of Justice/ITT Litigation.—US Senate Committee on the Judiciary, *Nomination of Richard Kleindienst to Serve as Attorney General of the United States, Hearings*, p. 17.

[38] For information on the ITT and Chile see US Senate, Subcommittee on Multinational Corporations of the Committee on Foreign Relations, 93rd Congress, *The International Telephone and Telegraph Company and Chile, 1970–71:* Sampson, *The Sovereign State of ITT:* US Senate Committee to Study Government Operations with Respect to Intelligence Activities, staff report, *Covert Action in Chile*.

[39] US Senate, Ervin Committee Hearings, Phase II, *Campaign Financing, p. 5471.*

[40] Ibid., p. 5495. See also *New York Times*, 10 Feb. 1977.

[41] US Senate, Ervin Committee, Phase III, *Campaign Financing* p. 5447.

[42] Epstein, op. cit.

[43] See Edward M. Epstein, 'Business and Labor in the American Electoral Process. A Policy Analysis of Federal Regulation—the Rise of the Political Action Committee', in Herbert E. Alexander (ed.), *Sage Electoral Studies Yearbook*, Vol. v, 1979: 'Corporate PACs Chart a Course through Congress' *Washington Monthly*, October 1978.

[44] *New York Times*, 16 May 1976.

[45] *Time*, 18 Dec. 1978, p. 27.

[46] *Congressional Quarterly Weekly Report*, Vol. xxxvi, No. 31, 'The Right in Congress Seeking a Strategy', p. 2022.

[47] *Washington Monthly*, October 1978.

[48] *Congressional Quarterly Weekly Report* Vol, xxxvi, p. 2205.

[49] Ibid., p. 2024.

[50] *New York Times*, 5 Feb. 1977 and 16 Jan. 1977.

[51] 'The Chamber and the NAM—A Marriage of Convenience', *National Journal*, 7 Aug. 1976. The marriage in fact was postponed.

[52] 'US Chamber Works to Erase Negative Image and Improve Grass Roots Clout', *National Journal*, 1 Apr. 1972.

[53] 'US Chamber and the NAM . . .', *National Journal*, op. cit.

[54] *National Journal*, 1 Apr. 1972.

[55] Ibid.

[56] Ibid.

[57] *National Journal*, 15 Apr. 1978.

[58] *Congressional Quarterly Weekly Report*, 'Business Round Table New Lobbying Force', 17 Sept. 1977.

[59] Ibid.

[60] Ibid.

[61] *Congressional Quarterly Weekly Report*, 11 Feb. 1978.

[62] *New York Times*, 7 Jan. 1979.

Chapter 5

[1] *Congressional Quarterly Weekly Report* xxxiv, no. 20, 15 May 1976, 'Public Interest Groups; Nader and Common Cause Become Permanent Fixtures'.

[2] Ralph Nader, *Unsafe at Any Speed*, Grossman, New York, revised ed. 1972.

[3] *Congressional Quarterly Weekly Report*, loc. cit.; Andrew MacFarland, *Public Interest Lobbies*, Decision Making on Energy, American Enterprise Institute, Washington DC, 1976. p. 45; Jeffrey M. Berry, *Lobbying for The People*, Princeton University Press, Princeton (NJ), 1977, pp. 27–34; *New York Times, 6 Feb. 1977*.

[4] *Congressional Quarterly Weekly Report*, loc. cit.

[5] Berry, op. cit., pp. 66–8; *Congressional Quarterly*, loc. cit.

[6] Mancur Olson, *The Logic of Collective Action*, Harvard University Press, Cambridge (Mass.), 1965.

[7] Berry, op. cit., p. 28.

[8] Ibid, pp. 39, 41.

[9] MacFarland, op. cit., pp. 4–24.

[10] Robert H. Salisbury, 'An exchange Theory of Interest Groups', *Midwest Journal of Political Science*, 13 (February 1969), pp. 1–32.

[11] Arthur Miller, 'Political Issues and Trust in Government', *American Political Science Review*, 63, (September 1974).

[12] Seymour Martin Lipset and William Schneider, 'How's Business?; What the Public Thinks', *Public Opinion*, Vol. 1, No. 13.

[13] Ibid.

[14] Berry, op. cit., p. 274.

[15] Gabriel Kolko, *The Triumph of Conservatism, A Re-Intepretation of American History, 1900–16*, Free Press of Glencoe Collier-Macmillan, London, 1963.

[16] MacFarland, op. cit., pp. 86–89.

[17] See, e.g., Kolko, op. cit.

[18] In the Social Contract Rousseau shows great suspicion of factions and interests. But he concedes that if any interests are to organize, all should; and by advocating rule by the General Will and not just majority vote, with a major effort to achieve unanimity, Rousseau hopes people may put aside their selfish concerns.

[19] MacFarland, op. cit., p. 3.

[20] United States Congress, Senate Subcommittee on Air and Water Pollution, Committee on Public Works, 91st Congress, 2nd Session, *Air Pollution 1970*.

[21] *Congressional Quarterly Weekly Report*, loc. cit.

[22] Ibid.

[23] *National Journal, 4 Dec. 1976*.

[24] *Congressional Quarterly Weekly Report*, op. cit.

[25] See above, chapter 4.

[26] 'Nader Nader?' *National Journal*, 17 Dec. 1977.

[27] *New Republic*, May 1979.

[28]Robert Sherrill, *Saturday Night Special*, Charterhause, New York, 1973.

[20] Richard Fenno, *Homestyle*, LittleBrown & Co., Boston, 1977.

Chapter 6

[1] *Lester W. Milbrath, The Washington Lobbyists*, Rand McNally, Chicago, 1963, pp. 179 ff.

[2] Angus Campbell, Philip Converse, Warren Miller, and Donald Stokes, *The American Voter*, John Wiley & Co., New York and London, 1964.

[3] V. O. Key, *Politics, Parties and Pressure Groups*, Thomas Crowvell & Co., New York, 1964.

[4] Ibid., p. 522.

[5] Anthony King, 'Ideas, Institutions and Policies', *BJPolS* 3 (1973), summarizes the literature well. See Theodore Marmer, *The Politics of Medicare*, Routledge & Kegan Paul, London, 1970.

[6] Arthur Kornhauser, Harold L. Sheppard, and Albert J. Mayer, *When Labor Votes*, University Books, New York, 1956.

[7] Perhaps the seniority system and the Rules Committee were more important as defences for legislators than barriers to their wishes. See Barbara Hinckley, *The Seniority System In Congress*, Indiana University Press, Bloomington and London, 1971, and James A. Robinson, *The House Rules Committee*, Bobbs-Merrill, Indianapolis, 1963, for proof that neither seniority nor the Rules Committee regularly frustrated majority opinion.

[8] Warren Miller and Donald Stokes, 'Constituency Influence in Congress', *APSR* lvii. 1 (March 1963).

[9] Raymond Bauer, Ithiel de Sola Pool, Lewis Anthony Dexter, *American Business and Public Policy*, Atherton Press, New York, 1963.

[10] Ibid., p. 398.

[11] Joseph Goulden, *The Super Lawyers*, Dell, New York, 1973.

[12] Milbrath, op. cit., p. 143.

[13] US Senate, Committee on Government Operations 94th Congress 1st Session, *Lobby Reform Legislation*, GPO, Washington DC, 1976, p. 44.

[14] *Kleindienst hearings.*

[15] US Senate, *Committee on Government Operations*, Hearings, op. cit. p. 231.

[16] Maurice Duverger, *Political Parties*, Methuen & Co., London, 1954.

[17] Bauer, Pool, and Dexter, op. cit.

[18] Milbrath, op. cit., p. 247.

[19] US Senate, *Committee on Government Operations*, Hearings op. cit., pp. 414–17.

[20] Ibid., pp. 45–6, testimony from John Gardner, Common Cause.

[21] Ibid., p. 2.

[22] Graham K. Wilson, 'Are Department Secretaries Really a President's "Natural Enemies"?', *BJPolS* 7, part 3, 1977.

[23] Hugh Heclo, 'Issue Networks and the Executive Establishment', in Anthony King (ed.), *The New American Political System*, A.E.I., Washington DC, 1978, and *A Government of Strangers*, Brookings Institution, Washington DC, 1977.

[24] G. William Dornhoff, *Who Rules America?*. Prentice Hall, Englewood Cliffs, N.J., 1967.

[25] Hugh Heclo, op. cit.

[26] Nelson Polsby, 'Interest Groups and the Presidency: Trends in Political Intermediation in America', in Walter Dean Burnham and Martha Wagner Weinberg (eds.), *American Politics and Public Policy*, MIT Press, Cambridge (Mass.) and London, 1978.

[27] *New York Times*, 4 Mar. 1979.

[28] Norman Nie, Sidney Verba, Petrocik, *The Changing American Voter*, Harvard University Press, Cambridge, Mass., 1975. Walter De Vries and Lance Tarrance Jr, *The Ticket Splitters: A New Force in American Politics*, Eerdmans, Grand Rapids, 1971.

Chapter 7

[1] I take it that this statement is uncontroversial. Important representatives of the pluralist paradigm were David Truman, *The Governmental Process*, Alfred Knopf, New York, 1951: Robert Allen Dahl, *A Preface to Democratic Theory*, Phoenix Books, New York, 1963, and *Democracy in the United States, Promise and Performance*, Rand McNally, Chicago, 1969.

[2] E. C. Schattschneider, *The Semi Sovereign People*, Holt Reinhard & Winston, New York, 1960.

[3] Mancur Olson, *The Logic of Collective Action*, Shocken Books, New York, 1969.

[4] Peter Bachrach and Morton Baratz, 'The Two Faces of Power', *APSR* 1962.

[5] Steven Lukes, *Power A Radical Interpretation*, Macmillan, London, 1974.

[6] Charles E. Lindblom, *Politics and Markets*, Basic Books, New York, 1977.

[7] There is an extensive literature on corporatism. The most convenient starting points are Phillipe Schmitter 'Still the Century or Corporatism?', *Comparative Studies*, 1 (1977), and Phillipe Schmitter and Gerhard Lehmbruch (eds.), *Corporatism* Sage, London, 1979. Vol. i (Vol. ii is due in 1980).

[8] See, e.g., G. K. Wilson 'Why there is no Corporatism in the United States', in Schmitter and Lehmbruch (eds.), Vol. ii: or Salisbury's piece ibid., Vol. i.

[9] For major studies casting considerable doubts on the power of interest groups see Raymond A. Bauer, Ithiel de Sala Pool, and Lewis Anthony Dexter, *American Business and Public Policy*, Prentice Hall International, London and New York, 1961. Lester Milbrath, *The Washington Lobbyists*. See also G. K. Wilson, *Special Interests and Policy-making* John Wiley & Son, London and New York, 1977.

[10] Werner Sombart, *Why there is No Socialism in the United States*, translated from the German by P. M. Hocking and C. T. Husbands, Macmillan, London, 1976.

[11] Norman Ornstein and Shirley Elder, Interest Groups—Lobbying and Policymaking', *Congressional Quarterly*, Washington DC, 1978, p. 23.

[12] See G. K. Wilson, *Unions in American National Politics*, Macmillan, London, 1979.

[13] Kliendienst hearings, p. 745.

[14] *New York Times*, 4 Jan 1976.

[15] US Senate, Select Committee on Campaign Practice, phase III, *Campaign Financing*, p. 5447.

[16] Andrew S. MacFarland, *Public Interest Lobbies*, American Enterprise Institute, Washington DC, 1976, provides the most cogent discussion. See also Jeffrey M. Berry, *Lobbying for the People*, Princeton University Press, Princeton, 1977.

[17] Berry, op. cit.

[18] *National Journal* 10 Apr. 1976; *Washington Monthly*, October 1978; Edward Epstein 'Business and Labor in the American Electoral Process, A Policy Analysis of Federal Regulation—The Rise of the Political Action Committee' in Herbert Alexander (ed.), *Sage Electoral Studies Yearbook*, Vol. v, 1979.

[19] *New York Times*, 16 May 1976.; *Time*, 18 Dec. 1978, p. 27.

[20] Edward Epstein, *The Corporation in American Politics*, Prentice-Hall Internationals, Englewood Cliffs, NJ, 1969; Bauer, Pool, and Dexter, op. cit.

[21] *National Journal* 15 Apr. 1978.

[22] *National Journal* 7 Aug. 1976; 1 Apr. 1972; *New York Times* 5 Feb. and 16 Jan. 1977.

Bibliography

Anderson, James, (ed.), *Politics and Economic Policy Making*, Addison-Wesley, Reading (Mass.), 1970.

Barbash, Jack, *The Practice of Unionism*, Harper & Row, New York, 1956.
Unions and Union Leadership, Harper & Brothers, New York, 1959.

Bachrach, Peter, and Baratz, Morton, 'The Two Faces of Power', *APSR* 1962.

Barkan, Al, 'Political Activities of Labor', in *Issues in Industrial Society*, Vol. 1, no. 2 (1969).

Barry, Brian, 'The Obscurities of Power', *Government and Opposition*, Vol. 10, 1975.

Bauer, Raymond, Pool, Ithiel de Sola, and Dexter, Louis Anthony, *American Business and Public Policy*, Prentice Hall International, London and New York, 1964.

Berger, Samuel R., *Dollar Harvest*, Heath Lexington Books, New York, 1971.

Berry, Jeffrey, *Lobbying for the People*, Princeton University Press, Princeton NJ., 1977.

Blauner, Robert, *Alienation and Freedom, The Factory Worker and his Industry*, University of Chicago Press, Chicago, 1964.

Bok, Derek, and Dunlop, John T., *Labor and the American Community*, Simon & Schuster, New York, 1970.

Brill, Stephen, *The Teamsters*, Simon & Schuster, New York, 1978.

Calkins, Fay, *The CIO and the Democratic Party*, University of Chicago Press, Chicago, 1952.

Campbell, Christina McFadyen, *The Farm Bureau and the New Deal*, University of Illinois Press, Urbana, 1962.

Crampton, J. A., *The National Farmers' Union, Ideology of a Pressure Group*, University of Nebraska Press, Lincoln, Nebraska, 1965.

Catchpole, Terry, *How to Cope with COPE; The Political Operations of Organised Labor*, Arlington House, New York, 1968.

Christenson, Les, *The Brannan Plan, Farm Politics and Policy*, University of Michigan Press, Ann Arbor, 1959.

Crenson, Matthew, *The Un-Politics of Air Pollution, A Study of Non-Decision Making in the Cities*, Johns Hopkins Press, Baltimore, 1971.

Dahl, Robert, *Who Governs?*, Yale University Press, New Haven, 1961.

Domhoff, G. William, *Who Rules America?*, Prentice Hall International, Englewood Cliffs, NJ, 1967.

Duscha, Julius, *Taxpayers' Hayride*, Little Brown and Co., 1964.

Edelstein, J. David, and Warner, Malcolm, *Comparative Union Democracy, Organisation and Democracy in British and American Unions*, George Allen & Unwin, London, 1975.

Engler, Robert, *The Brotherhood of Oil*, University of Chicago Press, Chicago and London, 1977.

Epstein, Edward M., *The Corporation in American Politics*, Prentice Hall International, Englewood Cliffs, NJ, 1969.

'Business and Labor in the American Electoral Process, A Policy Analysis of Federal Regulation—The Rise of the Political Action Committee', in Herbert Alexander (ed.), *Sage Electoral Studies Yearbook*, Vol. v, 1979.

Fenno, Richard, Jr., *Congressmen in Committees*, Little Brown and Co., Boston 1973.

Homestyle, Little Brown and Co., Boston, 1978.

Finley, Joseph E. *The Corrupt Kingdom*, Simon & Schuster, New York, 1972.

Fite, Gilbert, *George N. Peek and the Fight for Farm Parity*, University of Oklahoma Press, Norman, 1954.

Foner, Philip S., *Organised Labor and the Black Worker, 1619–1973*, Praeger, New York, 1972.

Galbraith, J. K., *American Capitalism, The Concept of Countervailing Power*, Hamish Hamilton, London, 1957.

Galenson, Walter, and Lipset, Seymour Martin, (eds.), *Labor and Trades Unionism, An Interdisciplinary Reader*, John Wiley and Sons, New York and London, 1960.

Goldberg, Arthur, *Labor United*, McGraw-Hill Co. Inc., New York, 1956.

Goulden, Joseph C., *Meany*, Atheneum, New York, 1972.

The Superlawyers, Dell, New York, 1973.

Greenstone, J. David, *Labor in American National Politics*, Alfred Knopf, New York 1969.

Guinther, John, *Moralists and Managers, Public Interest Movements in America*, Anchor Books, New York, 1976.

Hall, Donald R., *Co-Operative Lobbying, The Power of Pressure*, University of Arizona Press, Arizona, 1969.

Hamilton, Richard, *Class and Politics in the United States*, John Wiley & Sons, New York and London, 1968.

Harris, Richard, *A Sacred Trust*, Pelican Books, New York, 1969.

Decision, Ballantine Books, New York, 1971.

Harrod, Jeffrey, *Trade Union Foreign Policy*, Macmillan, London, 1972.

Heath, Jim F., *John F. Kennedy and the Business Community*, University of Chicago Press, Chicago and London, 1969.

Heclo, Hugh, *Government of Strangers*, Brookings Institution, Washington DC, 1977.

'Issue Networks and the Executive Establishment', in Anthony King (ed.), *The New American Political System*, American Enterprise Institute, Washington DC, 1978.

Hirschman, A. O., *Exit, Voice and Loyalty*, Harvard University Press, Cambridge (Mass.), 1970.

Holing, John, 'George Meany and the AFL-CIO', *New Republic*, Vol. 173 (1975).

Hutchinson, John, 'Labor and Politics in America', *Political Quarterly* (1962), p. 138.

James, Ralph and Estelle, *James Hoffa and the Teamsters*, Van Nostrand, Princeton, NJ, 1965.

Johnson, D. Gale, *World Agriculture in Disarray*, Fontana/Collins, London, 1973.

Josephson, Matthew, *Sidney Hillman, Statesman of Labor*, Doubleday & Co., New York, 1952.

Kampleman, Max, 'Labor in Politics', in *Interpreting the Labor Movements*, Industrial Relations Research Association, New York, 1952.

Kemble, Penn, 'Rediscovering American Labor', *Commentary*, Vol. 51, no. 4 (April 1971).

Kendall, Walter, *The Labour Movement in Europe*, Allen Lane, London, 1975.

Key, V. O., *Politics, Parties and Pressure Groups*, T. J. Crowell, New York, 1964.

Kile, O. M., *The Farm Bureau Through Three Decades*, Waverly Press, Baltimore, 1948.

Kolko, Gabriel, *The Triumph of Conservatism, A Re-Interpretation of American History 1900–16*, Free Press of Glencoe, Collier–Macmillan, London, 1963.

Kornhauser, Arthur, Sheppard, Harold L., and Mayer, Albert J., *When Labor Votes, A Study of Auto Workers*, University Books, New York, 1956.

Latham, Earl, *The Group Basis of Politics, A Study in Base Point Legislation*, Cornell University Press, Ithaca, 1952.

Levison, Andrew, *The Working Class Majority*, Coward McCann, Geohegan, New York, 1974.

Levitan, Sar A., (ed.), *Blue Collar Workers, A Symposium on Middle America*, McGraw-Hill, New York, 1971.

Lindblom, Charles E., *The Policy-Making Process*, Prentice Hall, New York, 1968.
   Politics and Markets; The World's Political-Economic Systems, Basic Books, New York, 1977.

Lipset, Seymour Martin, Trow, Martin A., and Coleman, James S., *Union Democracy, The Internal Politics of the International Typographical Union*, The Free Press, Glencoe, 1956.

Lord, Russell, *The Wallaces of Iowa*, Houghton Mifflin, New York, 1947.

Lukes, Stephen, *Power, A Radical View*, Macmillan, London, 1974.

McAdams, Alan K., *Power and Politics in Labor Legislation*, University of Columbia Press, New York and London, 1964.

McConnell, Grant, *The Decline of Agrarian Democracy*, University of California Press, Berkeley, 1953.

McCulloch, Frank, and Bernstein, Tim, *The National Labor Relations Board* Praeger, New York, 1974.

McCune, Wesley, *Who's Behind Our Farm Policy?* Praeger, New York, 1956.

MacFarland, Andrew, *Public Interest Lobbies Decision-Making on Energy*, American Enterprise Institute, Washington DC, 1976.

Malbin, Michael, *Parties, Interest Groups and Campaign Finance Law*, American Enterprise Institute, Washington DC, 1970.

Malone, Albert P., *Lawyers, Public Policy and Interest Group Politics* University Press of America, Washington DC, 1977.

Mansen, R. Joseph, and Cannon, Mark W., *The Makers of Public Policy.*

American Power Groups and their Ideologies, McGraw Hill, New York, 1965.

Marmor, Theodore, *The Politics of Medicare*, Routledge & Kegan Paul, London, 1970.

Marshall, F. Ray, *Labor in the South*, Harvard University Press, Cambridge (Mass.), 1967.

Mayhew, David R., *Party Loyalty Amongst Congressmen; The Difference between Republicans and Democrats 1947–62*, Harvard University Press, Cambridge (Mass.), 1962.

Milbrath, Lester W., *The Washington Lobbyists*, Rand McNally, Chicago, 1963.

Miller, Arthur, 'Political Issues and Trust in Government', *APSR*, Vol. 63, September 1964.

Miller, Robert, and Johnson, Jimmy D., *Corporate Ambassadors to Washington*, American University Center for the Study of Private Enterprise, Washington DC, 1970.

Nie, Norman, Verba, Sidney, and Petrocik, John, *The Changing American Voter* Harvard University Press, Cambridge (Mass.), 1973.

Nye, Russell B., *Midwestern Progressive Politics*, Michigan State University Press, 1959.

Olson, Mancur, *The Logic of Collective Action*, Harvard University Press, Cambridge (Mass.), 1965.

Oppenheimer, Bruce I., *Oil and the Congressional Process*, Lexington Books, Lexington (Mass.), 1974.

Ornstein, Norman, and Elder Shirley, *Interest Groups, Lobbying and Policymaking*, Congressional Quarterly Press, Washington DC, 1978.

Pelling, Henry, *A History of American Labour*, University of Chicago Press, Chicago and London, 1960.

Polsby, Nelson, 'Interest Groups and the Presidency: Trends in Political Intermediation in America', in Walter Dean Burnham and Martha Wagnar Weinburg (eds.), *American Politics and Public Policy*, MIT Press, Cambridge (Mass.) and London, 1978.

Radosh, Ronald, *American Labor and United States Foreign Policy*, Random House, New York, 1969.

Raskin, A. H., 'AFL-CIO: A Confederation?', *Annals of the Academy of Political and Social Science, The Crisis in the American Trade Union Movement*, Vol. 350 (November 1963).

Reed, Louis, *The Labor Philosophy of Samuel Gompers*, Kennikat Press, New York, 1966.

Richter, Irving, *Political Purpose in Trade Unions*, George Allen & Unwin, London, 1973.

Roberts, B. C., *Unions in America: A British View*, Industrial Relations Section, Princeton University, Princeton NJ, 1959.

Rogin, Michael Paul, *The Intellectuals and McCarthy, The Radical Spectre*, MIT Press, Cambridge (Mass.), 1967.

Salisbury. Robert, 'An Exchange Theory of Interest Groups', *Midwest Journal of Political Science*, 13 (February 1969), pp. 1–32.

Schattschneider, E. E., *Politics, Pressures and the Tariff*, Archon Books, New York, 1963.

　　The Semi Sovereign People, Holt, Reinhart Winston, New York, 1960.

Seidman, Harold, *Politics, Position and Power: The Dynamics of Federal Organization*, Oxford University Press, Oxford, 1970.

Selznick, Philip, *The T.V.A. and the Grass Roots: A Study in the Sociology of Formal Organisation*, University of California Press, Berkeley, 1953.

Shonfield, Andrew, *Modern Capitalism: The Changing Balance of Public and Private Power*, Oxford University Press, Oxford, 1965.

Taft, Philip, *Labor Politics American Style: The California State Federation of Labor*, Harvard University Press, Cambridge (Mass.), 1968.

    Rights of Union Members and the Government, Greenwood Press, Westport (Conn.) and London, 1975.

Talbot, Ross B., and Hadwiger, Don W., *The Policy Process in American Agriculture*, Chandler Publishing Co., San Francisco, 1968.

Tanenhaus, Joseph, 'Organised Labor's Political Spending: The Law and its Consequences', *Journal of Politics*, Vol. 16, 1954.

Truman, David B., *The Governmental Process*, Alfred Knopf, New York, 1951.

Tweeten, Luther B., *Foundations of Farm Policy*, University of Nebraska Press, Lincoln, Nebraska, 1970.

Tyler, Gus, *The Labor Revolution*, Viking Press, New York, 1966.

Vale, Vivian, *Labour in American Politics*, Routledge & Kegan Paul, London, 1971.

Widdick, B. J., *Labor Today*, Houghton Mifflin, New York, 1964.

    'Labor 1975: The Triumph of Business Unionism', *The Nation*, Vol. 221, No. 6 (6 Sept. 1975).

Wieck, Paul, 'Labor and the Democrats', *New Republic*, Vol. 168 (30 June 1973).

    'Labor's Al Barkan', *New Republic*, Vol. 168 (24 Mar. 1973).

Wilson, Graham K., *Special Interests and Policymaking, Agricultural Policies and Politics in Britain and the United States*, John Wiley & Sons, London, 1977.

    Unions in American National Politics Macmillan, London, 1977.

    'Department Secretaries: Are They Really a President's "Natural Enemies"?', *BJPols* 5 (1975).

Windmuller, John 'The Foreign Policy Conflict in US Labor', *Political Science Quarterly*, lxxxii. 2 (June 1967).

Yarmolinsky, Adam, *The Military Establishment*, Harper & Row, New York, Evanston and London, 1977.

Ziegler, Harman L., and Peak, Wayne G., *Interest Groups in American Politics*, 2nd edition, Prentice Hall, Englewood Cliffs, NJ, 1972.

Index